Dear Helen,
It's been such...ing
a pleasure k
you and havin
...at our table

Your sister
Christ,
Barbara

MW01610792

ISBN: 978-1-300-96985-3

Overcomer

The word *Overcomer* is important in the end times; it is mentioned frequently in the book of Revelation. The emphasis and reward are upon effort, intestinal fortitude, and perseverance. *"And, ye shall be hated of all men for my name's sake. But he that endureth to the end shall be saved."* The believer must fight the good fight of faith. There are struggles and persistence involved in New Testament living. These qualities are not unknown to champions. Eddie Arcaro, one of the greatest jockeys in history, winner of five Kentucky Derbies, lost his first 250 races.

On Wings
By B.J. Moss

Dedication

My book is lovingly written to
Glorify my Creator
to help the mentally ill
to shed light so that the body of Christ
will better understand how to heal
those in bondage in their mind
and Set them Free!

I could never ask for any greater blessings than my Son
and the experiences I have ministering.

My deepest gratitude goes to my friend and editor Cheryl
Ann and to Penny, who lovingly pitched in to help type
this book.

FORWARD

The story I'm about to tell is my journey through a lifetime of suffering with manic depressive, or bi-polar disorder. I began taking lithium carbonate at 21, and also had my first shock treatments at that age. Three of my siblings committed suicide and I have wanted to take my own life on a number of occasions. Drug therapy coupled with psychotherapy has enabled me to live a successful life, though it has been fraught with challenges. Because I am a lifelong Christian, I can say that it has been evident to me that God has helped me when there was no hope. I am a pastor's wife, now widowed, a graduate of Oral Roberts University and a minister in my own right, an accomplished artist and an amateur dancer with some choreographed programs to my credit.

My story cannot be told without giving some explanation as to the activity of demonic forces. Derek Prince's classic book on demonology, "They Shall Cast Out Demons," explains the source of many behaviors and disorders. The bible teaches that dark forces will battle against us during our life on earth. The bible book of Ephesians explains it this way:

"But our struggle is not against flesh and blood, but against the rulers, against the authorities, against the powers of this dark world and against the spiritual forces of evil in the heavenly realms."

(Ephesians 6:12, NIV)

I tell my story in hope of encouraging those readers who themselves have bi-polar disorder or some other mental illness, or who want to help a suffering loved one. With God, all things are possible.

Today, I live a happy, healthy life. I have close friends and an active church life. The beautiful residential care facility where I live allows me to conduct prayer meetings and to dance for the residents during scheduled events. I drive to St. Louis and visit the needy. My health is excellent and I have no physical problems. This is a testament to the power of God and the resources he has given us.

Family members of mine who are mentioned in this book, are treated with the utmost love and respect, and as graciously as possible. When Jesus was approached by a blind man, people asked him, "Who has sinned, this man or his parents?" and Jesus replied, "Neither, but that the Father may be glorified, this has happened."

Understanding as to the causes of bipolar disorder is ongoing. Having said that let us go back to my childhood in the Midwest, where my story begins......

1

Webster Groves

I was born on March 25, 1950. My mom, dad, brother Bob,
sister Linda, and I lived in St. Louis, Mo. When I was four,
we moved into a large, 100 year old farmhouse in Webster
Groves, Mo. This was the house I grew up in and where
my younger brother, Jim, younger sister Sally and younger
brother Don were born. It had a big porch that wrapped the
house Arcadian style. There was a beautiful foyer with a
grand front entry. The house had four bedrooms, three
downstairs and one upstairs, in the living room was a
wonderful hearth. A spacious dining room would
eventually accommodate all eight of us. The large kitchen
had four doors along one wall, each one leading
somewhere different, the pantry, outside, the basement and
upstairs. We thought it was so funny when someone
would go out the wrong door. You see my family was very
intelligent, all having high IQ scores. I could quote their
scores and there was some competition on that, more about
the competition later.

Getting back to the kitchen, the oblong table had a
ledge going around the perimeter where my siblings and I
would hide the food we didn't like, especially Brussels
sprouts. Mother would find them days later. In retrospect,
we were like typical kids in a typical family. Our basement
was really fun. I remember roller-skating and swinging
around the pillars. Though our large family was busy as
could be with many activities we helped each other the best
that we could. But I want to start with similarity or
'normality', if we might use that term. Like other families,
we had emergency stores in case of a tornado. Once I saw a

funnel cloud as we raced for the shelter. Ours was a fruit cellar which opened to the backyard, a common feature for many homes where canning took place.

In our large yard, at least it seemed large in my childhood; we had a tire swing and enough room to practice playing baseball. There were also enough trees for all the kids to climb. There was an attic we liked to play in by taking flashlights and exploring the dark passages while the floorboards creaked. It was all in the innocence of a child. But the world is often not 'child' friendly, and families have hurt one another since the fall in the garden, in Genesis. I became a product of the darkness we would descend into as one disaster after another affected family members and the 'normalcy' I craved during my childhood disintegrated. This was not a phenomenon I was equipped to rationalize nor could I admit to it as a child. All I could do was 'keep it together' tightly on the outside.

I remember an incident which happened one day on the front porch. As kids we put on 'parties' that entailed walking to the corner grocery and loading up on goodies and soda. Once I returned carrying a 6-pack of sodas. I was climbing the front steps behind my sister Linda and the bottom fell out of the bag, sending the soda bottles crashing to the ground. When Linda turned around to chastise me she saw me bleeding profusely, and she and my mother rushed to the car to take me to the hospital. The bleeding had to be stopped while we drove to the emergency room. I ended up with eight stitches. My three brothers Bob, Jim and Don all frequented the hospital with baseball injuries as we were growing up. Bob was the oldest, being seven years ahead of me. He taught me how to play baseball and we climbed trees together. We would all play freeze tag and other games with the neighborhood children.

My father had served in WWII. He married and became an employee of the Wagner Electric company. During the summer, for ten days, the whole family would go camping in his military issued tent to save money. Because he was an engineer and had a good job, we became a large family of eight. Mom would make homemade snow ice cream for all of us during the cold winter months.

Much of our world view as individuals is first shaped by our parents and siblings in childhood. What kind of mother or father we had, whether or not we were properly cared for, and the like. There is no shortage of hurt people and it may be that you yourself are one who is struggling for answers. Hopefully, my story will offer some aid.

At first, we have a profound need to find a place to lay the blame for our sorrows and short comings, and we need rational explanations. Go to any bookstore and you will find a wide selection of self-help books which attempt to help you vindicate your behavior, titillate your psyche, or provide neat phrases like 'co-dependency' to try and explain what happened. Psychotherapy is another option; the biblical world view, which you may not have been taught, offers hope and a means of understanding what could be explored. I can say this, because that's what ultimately helped me to be set free from unbearable pain and put a desire to live, live, live in my heart!

My siblings and I were not adopted. We were not given up at birth. We were not born with physical birth defects. We had a warm home, food to eat, and parents who engaged on some level with each of us. My father taught me to ride a bike. I helped my mother in the kitchen. After all, she had a large family to feed. My sister Linda would often be reading or practicing piano lessons. My brothers played ball, while my sisters and I had the usual interactions sisters have. I describe my family relationships because they are the people I lived with as a child. I could not tell the story of my life without detailing my sibling relationships and the personalities of my parents. They hold some degree of responsibility for my character formation and all relationships do affect us, just as we affect others. The history of my family will be a good place for you to begin to understand how my story may be similar to your own.

One of the gifts God has given me has helped me in so many ways. When I was very young, about 4 years old, I would follow my Mom to the kitchen, pull   on the hem of her skirt and plea, "Mommy Mommy, I want to take dancing! I was so persistent that she and my dad finally gave in and agreed to give me ballet lessons. Thera Pate, my ballet teacher, lived behind our house and across the railroad tracts. I would walk by myself holding a one dollar bill in my hand to give for my lesson. She had been a Rockette in New York City and was an excellent dance teacher. Her support for me was helpful and I respected her. Our relationship grew and she encouraged me to try out for the Muny Opera. Our family moved to Lynchburg Virginia and God took complete control of my destiny. The discipline, grace, confidence and coordination I had learned carried over into the rest of my life.

Jim, my brother four years younger, was an accomplished baseball player. He was a very good looking young man, with a medium build, beautiful blue eyes and dark hair. One day Jim brought home a puppy and our parents let him keep it. She was part Irish setter, part

11

German shepherd, cute and fluffy. Jim named her Dori. Thereafter my father would always say, "Everything is hunky-Dori at our house." This sounds like a harmless, even humorous statement. I'm sure my father meant it to be, whenever he uttered it. The great irony is that the exact opposite was true. Sadly, everything was most definitely NOT, 'hunky-Dori'. In my own family, the unfolding of events for its members would be wrought with pain, sorrow and despair. Though many people can to a greater or lesser extent, point to the painful circumstances they endured while living their life, some of us need more explanation as to why. Why did I, my family, have to endure so much pain? Others will say their life has been charmed; they never experienced disagreeable circumstances or sorrows. I don't think those people are really being honest.

For me, I chose to bear up under the burdens as they presented themselves and psychologists would say I took on a role of 'rescuer'. I could have chosen the role of 'victim', because we have the freedom to choose our response, but that would be unacceptable to my competitive nature. By virtue of our family's definition of success, I could not afford to adopt the victim stance. I would go on to accomplish amazing things in the midst of adverse circumstances. Human beings can often display amazing resilience, and outwardly that was my case. But eventually, I ran out of steam. I reached a point of 'disintegration', a psychological crisis. Not only did mental illness take hold of my siblings, but I battled with a desire to commit suicide. This seems to be a more common problem in the present times, but in that era, it was very real as well. To have several siblings who also had the same desire is beyond any conceivable norm, however. What had happened?

The bible teaches that we are created in the image of God, but because of Adam's sin in the Garden of Eden, we have become tarnished and fall far short of what God intended we should and could be. When I became a Christian, I learned that through the life and death of Jesus Christ, I could redeem that image and experience restoration and fulfillment in the face of horrible odds. Becoming a Christian gave me a new world view, a new hope, and the sense that when all is said and done, there is a reason to live.

It could be argued, and has, that some people are just misfits. The weak, the lame, physically handicapped, blind or mentally ill just do not fit neatly into society. Those who adopt this premise would like to sweep us all under the rug. Oh, there are lots of ways to do it. Hitler conducted the 'great experiment', and specifically targeted the mentally ill (in addition to the Jews), though society would like to forget. In earlier centuries, little was known about human psychology so unspeakable acts and misguided laws made life for mentally ill people unendurable, if not short. Given the varying degrees of mental illness, this could range anywhere from public jeers and ridicule, to absolute confinement or death. Thank God society has made leaps and bounds, at least in civilized and Judeo-Christian society, in the area of psychology and approaches to helping the growing numbers of mentally ill people. In some places, there is a partnership developing between these medical professionals, and religious leaders in the churches as they both seek to restore people to their greatest potential.

Alongside the craziness of the one who is mentally ill, myself in this story, normal life progresses along, well, normally. Though 'normal' is really a man-made construct

13

used to help define our world, and 'crazy' is a term used loosely these days. When someone is undergoing mental struggles, labels like that tend to create more misunderstanding. Another problem with labels is that they can become popular quite quickly as 'sound bites' to help explain difficult illnesses. They can be applied over zelously if care is not taken to dig down and learn what a particular individual is really suffering from. In the case of bi-polar disorder, it seems to rank second in popularity only to ADD or ADHD. These psychiatric disorders take on popular status which further complicates the lives of people who really are struggling with legitimate mental breakdown. They need more understanding, and less labeling.

I am thankful for the ability to recall many of the flowers that bloomed in my life along the way. My family and I tried many avenues; hospitals, doctors and medications over the course of my illness. I was a youth when the illness initiated, and now I am in my 60's. I have been taking lithium for decades, and other drugs before that. I've had shock therapy twice.

All along, my early childhood experience with Jesus through church attendance and youth group activities buoyed me up as a counterweight to the downward spiral which seemed always to be trying to suck me in. I cannot overstate the help Jesus Christ, my savior has rendered me. He brought me through whenever I was faced with serious challenges. His work in my life is an ongoing one, and the bible states we go *"from glory to glory"*, until we one day will meet Him face to face, and the bible says, '*we will be like Him*'.

One of my memories is of my little sister Sally.

When she came along, she was so cute. Eventually her platinum blonde hair would fall way down her back. She too had blue eyes and a cute figure so that I would joke and sing with her, 'Five feet-two, eyes of blue chubby dubby dubby du has anybody seen my gal?" Don, the youngest, was very well loved and I always looked out for him. I helped take care of him when he was a baby, changing his diapers, etc. Once, while putting him into the bassinet, I chirped 'Donald Duck!' to avoid hitting his head. It's funny the memories I recall. Of course there are many that I chose to forget. I remember Mom cooked the meals and I did the baking to help her. I still love to bake.

When I was still in grade school, our family was becoming involved with the local Disciples of Christ church. We joined the youth softball team, and some of us sang in the choir. One day I heard the gospel presented in Youth Fellowship and I surrendered my life to Jesus, on my knees at my bed. I made him my Lord and Savior. My life was totally changed and I noticed a new compassion for the lost and needy of this world. God was preparing me for a life of service. This goal would influence all my choices and would offer me grounding in something stable amidst the emotional chaos that often characterized my life. God began to build in me a compassion for those who struggled within their own minds. The bible speaks of 'those who oppose themselves in their own minds.' I would go through these struggles as well. That gave me a real framework through which to bring the Grace of God to those who had been cast off from 'neat society' and housed in facilities known as sanitariums, psych wards, institutions, nut houses, etc. where they were medicated with dosage levels that proved to be too high, sometimes experimental psychotropic drugs, and minimal or ineffective counseling necessarily required to build the package needed for progress. Freud may have provided some technical analysis and expertise, but drug therapy was still developing in the early sixties. I've undergone psychiatric therapy, Christian counseling, psychological evaluation, and tests of all kinds. During the decades of my life where I've struggled to recover I've gotten a wider perspective. Let's get back to the beginning.

During my youth, my high school was chosen as a model for others and it ranked one of the best in the nation. Cameramen showed up to film a tape for the 'Lucas Tanner' show. A documentary was also produced named "Sixteen in Webster Groves". This kind of excellence impressed me and our family and motivated me to excel in all I did. I received scholarships and promotions throughout my life and career for top performance. As a Christian, too, it was very important for me to choose the moral high ground. Later on, one reason I didn't join a sorority was for their selection process, which was elitist. They excluded those who weren't good enough. So there is a dichotomy in that I felt I performed in a superior way, yet I had the utmost compassion for those who didn't measure up. It may have been that my manic states contributed to the drive and achievement while the depressive or calm state allowed me to identify with others who were feeling low.

After becoming 'born again' by making Christ head of my life at around the age of 15, it became apparent that I loved serving people in many ways. When I was 12 years old, there was a mental health institute down the street on Grant Road where I volunteered to help the elderly. I would take walks with them, water their plants and perform personal grooming. At fourteen, I was a candy striper at St. Joseph's Hospital near my home. I found it very rewarding to help the nurses with their patients. One

16

incident, however, was markedly traumatic. I was feeding an elderly man who was telling me all about his life as an undertaker, when all of a sudden the sound of a gunshot went off across the hall. Quickly, I ran to the room to find a woman holding a gun, and blood streaming from her forehead. Suddenly, a nurse came up from behind and swept me away, hoping to guard me from the horror, but of course it was too late.

As a girl scout I earned many training badges in disciplines that would aid me throughout life. I was elected secretary of my Methodist Youth Fellowship (MYF). The pastor asked me to lead the prayer during an MYF youth service at our church. Within this group we had chaperoned dating and mission projects.

At home, things were not peaceful. My father would be mentally exhausted when he came home from work at the electric company. He would go straight to the television to watch the nightly news. No one could think of disturbing him. We knew better. We did our best to honor his needs although we would have liked to spend more time with him. When my oldest brother, Bob, or my mom came into the room, dad would let loose with irritation. In his anger he would yell to the point of distressing family members. My father had an anger problem, but in those days people did not recognize this as an issue to be dealt with. Two world wars had affected the culture in its own way. Veterans often struggled with their own inner demons, and there were not many answers available as to how to deal with them. I use the term 'demons' here in the common sense similar to the saying 'having a monkey on your back', but this saying may well be rooted in the actual existence and appearance of demons. It is now understood that severe or prolonged trauma can be a catalyst which initiates the onset of certain types of psychiatric disturbances. Demons, which world religions recognize, and which Christ came to defeat, will torment people and hold them captive to these painful events and even try to intensify their painful impact on a person's life. Jesus' earthly ministry, before his crucifixion and resurrection was often occupied with the casting out of demons. He himself stated this as one of the purposes of his coming into the world.

So I was the middle child. I became the peace maker and co-dependency began to creep into my life. I would sometimes position myself between my parents as the 'diplomat', for it seemed my mother was too paralyzed to act. She played a passive role in this area of our home-life. My mother's mother, my maternal grandmother, died in childbirth and my mother was raised by her father for several years, and then by a stepmother. She was a wonderful mother. Therefore, my mom was also a very good mother, just too busy!

In the 10th grade my history teacher assigned a 60 page term paper. I stayed up into the early morning hours working on it and the combination of extra activities, home stress and schoolwork took their toll in the form of a breakdown. To be truthful, I felt compelled to complete my assignment and looking back, I should've expressed my need for help. Mom took me to the family doctor and he checked me into the local hospital for observation. Though I could not even lift my hands from the chair, they found nothing wrong with me. Here is an example of the inadequacy of the medical establishment at that time (60's) to grasp or diagnose the underpinnings of mental trauma or personality breach. There was another event during my 10th grade year which may have precipitated the breakdown. I was very close to my maternal grandfather,

Grandpa Stephens. I learned about Christianity from his reading the bible to me on his lap. He had an inner strength which helped him throughout life. I observed his gentleness. His wife had died when my mother was born, so he raised my mother as best he could until he remarried when my mother turned six. His death and the funeral represented the first relative whose death I mourned because he gave generous affection that my parents didn't have time to give to me.

Many people will attribute lack of parental affection to be at least partially, the cause of their problems, but even taking into account differences in degree, all human beings have a deep need to be loved for who they are, with all our imperfections. Without an encounter with the unconditional love God intends for us, we go through life feeling somewhat short-changed. The hospital could find nothing wrong after this incident. Perhaps it should be stated at this juncture that medical insurance at the time may have been inadequate to cover illnesses that were not yet fully recognized as legitimate in the sense of biologically curable, or worthy of setting aside funds. So I received no care and went on to 'wing it' as they say, for the time being. But life didn't slow down and wait for me to get help and the stress increased.

During this time period my mother also had to go to the hospital for a hysterectomy. In those days women were hospitalized for several weeks for this procedure. It is traumatic enough in itself. Few doctors explain the real impact of such a profound altering of the female reproductive system, with all its attendant systems, including endocrine, lymph, etc. My older sister was going to go off to college in Nashville so I was the logical stand-in to help my father with the other siblings. God gave me the stamina to take care of things. Jim, Sally and Don were about 11, 10 and 7 years old at the time. I cooked the meals and dad was very appreciative. I recall he did not yell as much as usual. I don't know what to attribute this to, except to say that he may have been grieving or somehow experiencing concern over his wife's hospital ordeal. He depended a great deal on my mother. I really enjoyed the role of caretaker for my siblings. My mother's friend checked in on us a few times.

2

Virginia

We moved to Lynchburg, Virginia when dad got a very prestigious job as chief engineer at H.K. Porter. That was to be the location of our family when illness struck me hard. Not only myself, but one after another of my siblings were having episodes of depressive and manic behavior. We became more aware of mental illness in our family.

For example, my brother Bob joined the Air Force at age 17 and left for Biloxi, MS. Six weeks into the rigorous program he collapsed and had a nervous breakdown. He was given an honorable discharge and sent home. I remember how I hurt for him. I was ten years old. After recuperating, Bob went off to Drury College in Springfield, MO. He returned home after one semester because of difficulties. He had little support and very low self-esteem. He would spend years trying to find his way.

By the time I was 17 years old, I was realizing how important communication was for healthy relationships. My dad believed in just sweeping everything under the carpet and pretending nothing was wrong, saying, 'Everything is Hunky Dori at our house." I wanted to please God more and more and I felt there was more to life than what I saw; I wanted to learn more about God's truth. I also wanted to say 'no' to dad's plans to move me to Virginia. Of course I was not allowed to express this, and if I had, dad would not have listened. You just didn't question dad. Many families during that era operated this way.

Because of the move to Lynchburg, I was not able to graduate with my class in Webster Groves. I had to take an additional year of high-school because all my credits didn't transfer.

Resulting from the lack of attention to my growing mental illness, I had two manic episodes in Lynchburg. I had a nervous breakdown while dancing in the community production of 'The King and I'. Juggling my many home and school duties, I learned there were limits, even for me. This is common for those with bi-polar disorder when in the manic state. They tell themselves, "I can do it all", because, on the inside, they feel like they have to. The alternative is a complete meltdown of the inner construct of family and self, or so they believe. Whether that is their real or a 'felt' position is something they cannot afford to discover. Such is the mental jail, or 'bondage' we are held in. To the extent that our psyche or rational self is incapacitated in this way, is the extent to which mental illness will manifest. The degree of infringement upon the ability to live life normally, or under reasonable circumstances, will determine whether or not medication, psychotherapy, counseling or institutionalization is recommended. I spent ten weeks in Radford, Va. in a psychiatric hospital. I became a candidate for medication. Mental issues had hospitalized various family members, including myself at least four times. Currently, there are leaps and bounds of progress in the field of mental illness, so that individuals who, in past decades, would remain in an institution with little progress, in some cases undergoing experimental drug therapy, could, under current conditions, recover and lead productive lives. The church, though a religious institution, has now come alongside the medical establishment as they both seek to learn from the other. Psychology Today, a popular magazine in that field, reported that drugs and therapy alone was often a temporary fix and that recidivism is an issue. Doctors who attended church began to look there for answers, and to look for ways to bring their discoveries into the clinical setting. One such individual is Francis McNutt whose medical experience with the military and subsequent call into the priesthood, combined to give him great counseling insight which has proven successful and effective. His book on healing, of the same title as the magazine "Psychology Today" is a bestselling classic.

Eventually, I got out of the psychiatric hospital, and continued on with educational and ministry goals, but this was not to be the end of my ordeal with mental illness. My siblings, as well, were fighting their own battles and sadly, three would succumb to their desire to take their own life and commit suicide. Dealing with their deaths and the less than meaningful funerals and interment decisions made by my parents just added to my sorrow. This was a modern-day tragedy, fit for some media crime feature.

True to my drive for perfection, but not without help from God, I received an academic scholarship from a Methodist school in west Georgia called La Grange. Three of my friends were already going there. So I embarked on a minister's journey which in itself is a testament to the grace and power of God working in my imperfect life. I think of 'Alice in Wonderland' and see a metaphor for my youth inhabiting different psychological venues which do not make sense, but the little bottle would at least allow me to navigate amidst the chaos. Who knows what the author had in mind when he wrote that classic story? An author once penned, "It was the best of times, and it was the worst of times...." which accurately describes my life as it were.

Leaving home for college was not to be a problem for me because my dad had become habitually angry, especially toward my brother Bob. I looked forward to getting away from it. Bob would eventually do the same.

3

College Years

La Grange was a Christian college and it was where I met my husband, Paul. We met before classes even started. I was instantly attracted to him and later learned of his Christian character. He said that he fell in love with my servant heart when I held his tennis shoes during the relay races at freshman orientation. Our first date was seeing the movie 'Romeo and Juliet.' Our courtship was sweet. We danced at the freshman prom, kissed all the time — and got called out for it. One day, two men I did not know told me, "You and Paul are as brother and sister and he will be unfaithful to you," and I never saw them again. We became serious about Paul's ministry calling and studied the Bible together for hours a day. He came to the point where he simply said, "Barbara, it's God's will for us to be together in marriage." That fall we shared hotdogs and popcorn together as we caught the Auburn College football games.

We decided to seek an institution where serious Bible students could avoid the drinkers and partying that characterized other colleges. We applied for scholarships to Oral Roberts University where Paul got full academic and I received both art and academic which covered almost all our college expenses. I obtained another scholarship after working in a nursing home because I ministered healing to the elderly there. Paul became a theology major, while I chose art and education.

While attending Oral Roberts, I became baptized in the Holy Spirit. God warmed my heart and brushed it with the wind of his Spirit. This was another step toward fulfilling my own ministry call. Upon finishing the first semester of our sophomore year, in 1970, I was weak from exams and went home to Lynchburg to rest over Christmas break. However, I did not get the rest I needed. Dad was continually haranguing Bob and would not leave him alone. I couldn't sleep and before I knew it I ended up at Duke University hospital in North Carolina. I remember mom coming in to wordlessly empty my dresser drawers as she packed my bags. No hugs or words of assurance were forthcoming. I attributed this to my mother's mom having died and further rationalized that dad didn't know how to demonstrate love. I believed his parents were cold and calculating. These are the answers we search to understand in therapy, whether in a psychiatric setting, or through Christian biblical counseling. I was no different than others who still find themselves hurting over family dysfunction, personal sin, and life in a fallen world.

Ever the diplomat, I found myself trying to make up the difference for what I perceived the family lacked in relational skills. The affection I would receive as I reached out to others taught me to reach out to my own family. I wrote letters to my father, and later found one of them on his bed stand that I had written him from La Grange College. I had thanked him for being a good provider for our family. Because I felt thankful that he had kept this letter it made me cry. I realized that somehow I may have gotten my message through.

Upon my arrival at Duke Hospital they stabilized me and put me on lithium carbonate. I was 21. The drug had been approved for use in Europe, much earlier, after its discovery in Australia. The Food and Drug Administration in the USA, had to put this drug, like all others, through its approval process, which could take a long time. They kept me for weeks to monitor the medicine. This was the same year I got my first shock treatments. After a time I was ready to go home.

When I was leaving, the psychiatrist acknowledged my good works while on the ward. I had reached out to others, even in my own time of need. Perhaps this is not the best situation or time to try and help others; however, that is what I did. I would traverse the hallways to talk and pray with individuals as God laid them on my heart. Anyway, the psychiatrist held a meeting with 12 interns where I was questioned but they didn't want to hear about my zeal for God. When I told them Jesus was the reason I was helping the others, they all rose from their chairs and filed out of the room. Psychiatry would not yet understand that some mentally ill patients do not have a 'martyr complex' or think they themselves are Jesus Christ. There are Christians who struggle with mental illness, yet love and serve their God.

Lithium had just been approved for use in the USA that year (1970). An Australian psychiatrist named John Cade had pioneered the discovery and use of the mineral lithium carbonate in treating mental illness while working at a mental hospital in Melbourne. For those who are interested, there was a documentary in 2004 called "Troubled Minds—the Lithium Revolution", which explains what a breakthrough the drug became for treating mania, severe depression, epilepsy and other illnesses upon its discovery. At the time, it revolutionized the field of mental health treatment.

Well, my brother Bob finally left home and went to California. He was able to obtain disability for mental illness and later had part-time jobs. Bob struggled in his own way during those years, trying to win dad's approval I

27

suppose, as most sons do. Bob took his own life in 1989.

I became restored enough to go back to Oral Roberts University in January 1971. Paul still loved and wanted to marry me. My roommate that semester was exhibiting antagonistic behavior toward me. The girl had a lot of anger and said her father was always yelling a lot. She would throw things around the room and I would run out in the hall to look for refuge. Take note that many of the situations I found myself in would involve flying objects and bizarre behavior, including my Christian marriage. In the case of this roommate, I expressed love toward her enough to receive a letter from her six weeks after graduation, thanking me for helping her and encouraging her to seek forgiveness in Jesus Christ. She became born again as a result. My life seemed inhabited by the mentally afflicted.

In the spring of 1972, I made plans for a mission trip to France with Youth With a Mission (YWAM). We had a 23 member team led by Joe Portali. He led us in humility and love, while we followed in meekness and respect. God's glory fell upon us and flowed through us. It seemed as if everything we did was fruitful. We shared testimonies and helped plant a church. During this trip I met Father Andrew, the well-known smuggler of Bibles into Russia. Paul was on mission in Germany. The mail was not getting through to us. I became despondent over not receiving letters from any of my loved ones. I prayed and received a comforting dream and experienced the unconditional love of Jesus Christ. It seemed I saw his face with light beaming from it. I will never forget this love. Before returning home, I was able to spend three nights in Germany with a traveling companion whose family allowed us to stay on their farm and they took us to visit magnificent castles. We also spent a day in Paris, France.

Paul and I went on to graduate with honors from the university. We decided we would marry immediately after the ceremony, partly to save money. The family members were driving in from St. Louis and Albany, Georgia. Pat Boone was the baccalaureate speaker and there was a torrential downpour which wet my hair. After my sister pinned it up and all the wedding party was in place, the service began. We took communion with the university chaplain. The ring I gave to Paul was a family heirloom engraved with, "Each for the other and Both for God." It had been my maternal great grandfather's who was a Methodist minister. By sunset we were beginning the reception. These were beautiful times in my life. Meanwhile, our zeal for God had increased as a result of the mission in Europe.

For now, Paul had to be in Dallas, Texas to attend Perkins School of Theology on the Southern Methodist University campus. We drove a 1969 Maverick. For this reason our honeymoon (which we won at the Oklahoma State Fair) where we stayed at beautiful Bella Vista resort in northwestern Arkansas for just five days hiking and sunning at the lake seemed too short. When we arrived at the campus, it was early May. I landed a teaching job that required me to teach two classes of French along with five classes of art instruction and they gave me a budget to start up an Art Department for the school. I had to study every night and brush up on my French. Each night I fell into bed exhausted. This was a repeating cycle for me, of stress, endurance, more stress and breakdown.

Later I was driving and almost got killed by another driver, who had sped up behind me. Since this was traumatic for me, we decided to move closer to the church and for me to walk to work. An elderly woman rented us an upstairs apartment at a good price. She was a seamstress for Mexican missions, stitching a dress each day. She and I watched the television show, 'The Waltons' together. She became like extended family to me during this long time living so far away from my own family. She had a window into our lives as a close friend. She once remarked that Paul was the 'little boy grown tall' because of some of his immature ways. Perhaps she was trying to tell me something, or maybe I am hinting at something in this memory. Later, it will become evident that flaws in relationships can sometimes become cracks.

One time I was in the bathroom and I looked up into the mirror, turned my head and saw a hideous creature like a gargoyle. I believe it was a demon of Lust. I turned to the mirror again, and then turned my head again and saw Paul standing there. Christianity throughout the ages has recognized the effects of spiritual activity in people's lives that is demonic. There are no rational explanations for them. They are supernatural in nature. The church deals with demons according to the teachings of Christ and the church proceeds to cast the demons out thru exorcism or deliverance. I am convinced I saw a demon manifestation by spiritual discernment, as the Bible teaches. For my part, I had also developed an ungodly belief that all men wanted was sex, but a biblical understanding would set me free from this.

At the time, I chose to ignore a lot of these things. There was far too much activity in our lives for me to pause. By now Paul had gotten a part-time job teaching Hebrew at Christ for the Nations and he was doing well. He still had to be encouraged because of his lack of confidence when teaching in front of a classroom. He was also sleeping so soundly, I had to physically rouse him from sleep on a regular basis. It seemed I had to bounce up and down on his chest at times to awaken him.

When my brother Bob came to visit us we bought our first TV at a yard sale. Bob really liked Paul and he stayed for a while. We had many laughs over dinner, including about the 'color television' being a 'pink and white'. When Bob had to leave I got sad and Bob took it hard as well. He was my older brother and I'd had so much compassion on his plights. These were a few cherished moments I choose to recall.

4

Seminary Days

That school term, the principal of the school started piling extra work on me for no extra pay. I held an art fair, painted, built scenery for the drama team. Since I was walking to and from the school in the cold, I got a very bad ear infection. During this time we had no health insurance. I called in sick, but as there was no substitute I went ahead in to work. That was a mistake and Paul later ended up taking me to the hospital. They wouldn't admit me, but gave me a prescription for a sleep aid. I lost my job and since we needed financial support so Paul could finish two more years of seminary, we transferred to Atlanta, Ga., to Emory University.

Paul planned a trip for us and 21 of his Hebrew students to travel to Israel and live on a kibbutz. These function as co-ops where everyone contributes to the community with their various skills and provision. Since it was imperative that my lithium be regulated, a necessity when taking this drug as it affects salt and fluid levels in the body with prolonged use, I was anxious over Paul's decision to flush my medication down the toilet. He would go on faith and I would go 'cold turkey' to Israel. Seems I didn't have much choice.

We moved everything we had to Georgia, which wasn't much because we had no furniture. We drove to Albany in our Ford Maverick, to his parent's house. Temperatures were high and we had radiator trouble along the way. Making that long trip in a less than suitable car presented its own challenges. When we had car problems, a man recommended that we put in 100 percent antifreeze. We were able to make the long drive after all. At one point Paul said to me, "Did you feel that?" Yes! We knew that God had performed a miracle by 'pushing the car' from behind. We met the other members of our team in New York City where we departed for Israel from John F. Kennedy airport.

God sustained me over the 10 week stay on the kibbutz during my withdrawal from lithium. We got up at 4:00 every morning and reported to work by 4:30. The land is arid so it didn't feel as hot without the humidity. I worked in the pear orchards, dining room and the cotton fields with some of the other students. I wasn't sleeping because I struggle with insomnia and some nights I didn't sleep at all. I became very tired, but I developed worship during this time to obtain peace and tranquility for myself. I had to lean on God and get His strength. It seemed I began to get victory over the depression that was setting in, though I would cry when the pain in my head from not sleeping became unbearable. My eyes were bloodshot and I'd pull myself together to get to the mess hall for lunch each day. The reader may be able to see that I was not being properly cared for as an individual struggling with mental illness and perhaps I was being taken advantage of, even by my closest loved ones. This is one of the reasons outside support in the form of medical personnel, medications and counseling become necessary. As a Christian, I was struggling, though the bible teaches healing for anyone. Without question, faith in Jesus Christ to heal any aberration in character, mind or body is a worthwhile, achievable goal. However, abusive or volatile relationships must be dealt with as part of the recovery from mental illness in an individual's life. We exist as members of families, churches and communities. The mentally ill person is not to be ostracized except under the direst conditions. The Gadarean demoniac mentioned earlier was a danger to himself and others in the community until Jesus healed him. God gave me strength to endure and my times of worship with Him were my key to achieving peace.

Such was my state of mind that I was able to enjoy some of the sightseeing in Israel, including the Wailing Wall in Jerusalem. I actually saw a snow-white dove perched atop it. There were busy open markets lining the streets. In the 'Old City' or East Jerusalem, you can get cooked lamb meat which hangs under many canopies and there are vegetables and art you can purchase. We dined in the King David Motel, which was wonderful. We rode camels, but you have to watch out or you may get bitten. One day, while sailing on the Mediterranean Sea in a little boat, a wind came up and was so strong that the owner had to rescue us. I thanked God for saving our lives that day. Later, we stretched out on the beach in our sleeping bags. God's grace was evident to me in more ways than one.

We swam in the Dead Sea, in grottos, and caves, and also in the Gulf of Elat and in the Galilean Sea. From Israel you can see Saudi Arabia across the Red Sea. One day a man approached us with an iron rod, the weapon of choice for beating a Christian (convert). Paul greeted the man cheerfully with "Boker Tove" which means 'good morning' at which point the man put the rod down and walked away.

At night the skies were clear. There is no rain except in winter so no cloud or mist hides the stars. The Milky Way is a sight to see under those conditions. Riding the bus to Masada, we were the only non-Arabs. The little children just stared at us. As the ten weeks wound up, the director of the kibbutz addressed our group and she invited us to come back again anytime. Several of our students did come back a few years following and there were some Jewish people from the kibbutz that gave their lives to Christ. We had a lot of fun and worked hard. After our trip we returned to the United States and I was able to get back on my lithium.

5

Early Ministry in South Georgia

After completing seminary, Paul went to work for the Methodist denomination. The district superintendent of the church gave Paul an appointment in Cochran, Ga. southeast of Macon to finish out the year. The Methodist denomination typically reassigns pastors every four years, or at least they did at that time. This was why we moved around so much, as you will see. We were constantly uprooting and getting reestablished. Paul was the youth director and associate pastor. It was a great place for us with fond memories. Being a college town, we often had visitors at our church. Paul got to preach often and improved rapidly. I used my talents to minister to the children as the choir director and for the various holiday programs. That year the city of Cochran sponsored a community parade in which many churches participated. Our youth group designed and built a float and named it, 'Love Came Down at Christmas.' I was still painting the globe of the world when we had to swoop away to line up at the church. There was a Holy Spirit Dove touching down on America. Frankly, it was impressive. At Easter we had a live pageant in our church yard. What a power-packed (Holy Spirit power) year it was.

We learned a lot about working with teenagers. I worked part-time in the day care center in Atlanta where we lived during the week and we commuted on weekends. One time I was getting off the bus in Atlanta and a vicious dog was running straight at me. He was foaming at the mouth and looked like he was going to tear me up. I pointed my finger at him and said, "Get behind me Satan!" The dog turned around in his tracks and ran the other direction! The senior pastor we served under called us, "the most dedicated couple in the South Georgia Conference." It was partly due to something that happened while we were there, and of course also due to my industrious personality.

I learned not to take someone else's medicine, not to play your own doctor. At one Sunday morning church service I had become manic. Symptoms of mania include, partially, increased energy and over activity, sleeplessness, and delusions involving inflated self-esteem. This state can also be induced by prolonged sedative use, or withdrawal from certain drugs. All of these factors came into play over the years of my life. As stated, I started on lithium at 21, and have taken sedatives (sleep aids) to the present time. Anyway, on that particular Sunday, the Pastor tried to help stem my mania by giving me one of his father's pills. I took a small amount then went home to bed. Wow! That threw me for a loop! By Sunday night church I was flying high. I was in the fellowship hall with my friend Marvelle and got real talkative and silly. She said, "Barbara, I've never seen you this way, what's going on?" By the time we got to the church service, I was in a full-blown manic state. Halfway through the sermon I felt so wired that when we sang I started clapping out of control. Marvelle and her husband came to my aide. He was a pharmacist and went to get a shot to calm me down. Paul and the senior pastor prayed. I calmed down then slowly walked to the altar, got up on the communion table and made a fool of myself. I began asking the people if they knew Jesus. As I looked into the eyes of the college students I saw expressions of tender amazement. How would I ever live this down? On the way out of the church I asked the Pastor's son if he knew Jesus. Paul held my hand tightly as he and the Pastor walked me home.

Well, the next morning I was absolutely fine and went about my daily activities. When I showed up to lead the children's choir, the Pastor looked astonished and asked me if I was up to it. The whole episode was instructive of the hazards of trying to handle a situation without expert medical care. It is dangerous to take someone else's prescription because of the brain chemicals and their delicately balanced system. Anyway, instead of taking another prescription medicine I decided to sing more as a way of becoming more able to relax. I could walk down the sidewalks and sing, "Slow down you move too fast, you've got to make the morning last, just tripping down the cobblestones, da da da da da feeling groovy." I also chose to get a puppy. Pets give us unconditional love and are known for their healing qualities. I chose a puppy, but it turned out that its mother had a calcium deficiency and died. I named her Ginger because she was light tan. She was part poodle and smart as a whip. I taught her sixteen tricks, which she would perform in front of my friends. I called her a circus dog. Ginger become like a member of the family. She was so good for me. I took her everywhere with me. Sadly she got hit by a car when only two years old, a great loss, one of many in my life.

6

A Difficult Assignment

Paul was next appointed to a small town called Sycamore, Ga. That was even further south than Cochran. This time Paul was the pastor and he preached every Sunday. He liked that and excelled at it. However, the Sycamore assignment was difficult in every way. In September on an early morning phone call, my mom told me that my older sister Linda had taken her life. I fell to my knees saying, 'Jesus, Jesus, Jesus.' When I told Paul, he did the very same thing. It was about 6:30 am. Later my mom explained that Linda had taken an overdose of prescription drugs with alcohol. Linda had struggled all her life. She had been engaged long ago but broke it off. When I asked her to come to my wedding in 1973, she wouldn't, "I'm jealous of you," she said. Not many months before she had visited us in Cochran. When she got off the bus and burst into tears I welcomed her and showed her to her room. We knelt down and prayed together, and she said she knew Jesus. We had several happy days together. When the bus came for her to leave, I opened the door of our parsonage and as she left she said she knew Jesus and believed that she would go to heaven.

The memorial service was held in our old Webster Groves and was solemn and brief. Later, when I boxed up what little Linda had, I found a diary along with some personal items. What I read was, 'Dear diary, I'm afraid to get married because I'm afraid that my husband will turn out to be like my father." That brought tears to my eyes. So that's why she kept breaking up with her boyfriends. She had been dating a Jewish boy before her death and he called my aunt for counsel long after Linda's passing.

I mentioned that this church assignment was particularly difficult. There were other reasons. We didn't understand the resistance we were getting to our ministry. We discovered after we left that there were witch's covens located nearby. Merriam Webster's Collegiate Dictionary defines a coven as an assembly of thirteen witches working in league with one another. They are often assigned to churches or ministry leaders. Later, I would have a personal encounter with one such individual.

Paul was finishing up his seminary work, and just before his graduation I got a call from my mom saying my younger brother Jim had taken his life. We spent all our money that September getting to Linda's memorial service so we were not able to get back for Jim's funeral. That day our church had a picnic scheduled and I was in charge of relay races for all the children. Emotionally, it was very difficult for me to make it through.

Jim had been close to me because of our many shared experiences. He did struggle at times, but seemed to be doing better after his senior year of high school. He graduated from sports broadcasting school, but somehow lacked direction and motivation. He tried to take his life several times before he finally succeeded. Sometimes I feel like I could have saved his life, but I realized that's not how to think.

One time when I came home from college, Jim tried to take his life and was in the hospital so I went there. I had the opportunity to talk to him alone. They had pumped his stomach of the overdose and he was stabilized. This was a spiritually tender time for him and after I presented the plan of salvation through Jesus Christ to him, he gave his heart to Jesus and was radically changed. After that he wanted very much to please God and often asked me questions about the Christian life. He was also able to visit us for several days when we lived in Dallas. I am confident he is in heaven. However, I came to dread early morning calls from my mother.

It sometimes seemed as though our family was targeted by the devil (Satan). When so many deaths occur in one family, questions do arise. One time on the way to Atlanta to see us from St. Louis my mom fell asleep at the wheel and the car spun around to drive in the opposite direction. My mom, dad and younger brother would have been killed. I remember sitting at the graduation ceremony for Paul at Emory University Theological School with three saved seats. My family was very late and I became concerned. They finally arrived midway through the service and later mom confessed what happened. With a sigh of relief I hugged them and we took pictures of Paul with his diploma as I thanked God. My mother had been weak with grief and from consoling family members and just hadn't gotten the sleep she needed. The district moved us from there in 1976.

Our next assignment, again in Georgia, was in Cairo. We had a less than adequate parsonage, but were able to reach many people there. I began singing solos in church and found I enjoyed it. A local ballet teacher asked me to be her assistant, so every spring I helped put on the recital for students ages 3-14. I would often dance with them.

During this time Paul and I were also able to take a second honeymoon on pristine St. George Island, where we camped with sleeping bags. This was a much needed respite for us. We slept under a full moon and enjoyed the phosphorescent condition of the water as dolphins frolicked all around us as we swam there. Our car got stuck in the sand, and we laughed as we pushed it out. Paul caught a jellyfish.

When I was hospitalized in Albany, Georgia, during our Cairo assignment, I had a real encounter with a witch. My husband had just visited me and was driving home but felt alerted somehow by the Holy Spirit, to call the hospital and insist that they keep an eye on me. They didn't. In my room I was standing at the hospital window looking out and already missing Paul when behind me arose a force that was unexplainable. I was finding myself opening the screen and then wanting freedom. Yes, freedom from my long struggle with sickness. I actually believed that if I jumped out of the window that I would be free. I got up on the windowsill and jumped. I was on the second floor of the psychiatric ward! God had his hand on me. I landed on my feet. The only injury was that I hit my head on a concrete slab and blood was gushing out. I walked around the building to the emergency room and immediately they grabbed me and put me on a stretcher and sewed up my head. I got thirteen stitches. They escorted me back to the ward. I also split my wisdom tooth in half and had to have it extracted. Right after I got up to my room I was sitting on my bed and a cute young lady bounced into my room. She plopped herself right down next to me and said, "I am a witch and I'm the one who made you jump out of that window." Immediately I stood up, pointed to the door and stated forcefully, "Get out of my room, now." She left and I began praying in the Spirit. I did this for about 20 minutes, praying in tongues as I was led. After I felt at peace, I called Paul. He was angry with the hospital's lack of supervision. The hospital paid my bills and released me soon afterward.

In Cairo we planted a huge vegetable garden, applying what we'd learned on the kibbutz in Israel. We had tomatoes, potatoes, turnips, green beans, etc. I bought a Vitamix machine and ground wheat for homemade bread. We also gleaned blueberries. Blue berries are good for the brain, incidentally. We shared our produce with church members and neighbors.

That spring the dance troop I was involved with was putting on a recital. The entire program was 2 ½ hours long and I believe I was the only Christian dancer. I chose a piece called, appropriately, "He Is Risen." We performed in the local high-school auditorium, which was not air conditioned. God blew a breeze through and many were touched, judging by their responses. My husband missed the recital because he was preparing a funeral message for a Vietnam veteran. So many people attended the funeral and Paul's message was outstanding. Then we began to feel called to a bigger congregation. At the time, the Methodist denomination did not recognize the charismatic gifts displayed by the Holy Spirit. We were attending a bible study with other believers that were full gospel, or all-inclusive as far as the Holy Bible is concerned. One funny thing happened at a board meeting in our parsonage that gave some comic relief. We were gathered around our dining room table and a 4yr. old child bounds into the room exclaiming, "You turkeys just do it!"
I also heard a cute joke. A ministerial family came home from church, as the mother put the food on the table, the father told the kids to wash their hands. His son stomped into the bathroom saying, "Germs and Jesus, germs and Jesus, that's all I ever hear around here and I ain't seen one

of them yet!!!"

7

David's Miracle Birth

In our sophomore year of college Paul shared a prophecy with me, he had received it that morning.

"We would have a son named David, and he will be a child of peace."

Our fourth to last assignment was in Blakely, near the Alabama state line. Though the scriptures were presented with drama and skill, the small country town did not appreciate them. Because of my mental health problems and having to be on medication to live a normal life, we had put off starting a family. The doctors had told me almost a year before that I was making medical history by overcoming my sickness. My doctor was gradually weaning me off my medication (lithium, etc.). By January of 1981 I was to be medication free. Paul and I talked about having our first child soon after that. The Lord had different plans! In September I started taking vitamin E for some small cysts I had and it threw my system off. I got pregnant in the middle of October. Paul and I were overjoyed! We danced around our living room when I found out the pregnancy test was positive. I called my doctor and he said that I could stop taking the medicine at this point and I would do just fine.

I had a very enjoyable pregnancy and felt good the whole time. I kept my weight down and exercised. In the middle of the pregnancy the Lord reminded me of the scripture, *"Notwithstanding she shall be saved in child bearing, if they continue in faith and charity and holiness with sobriety."* (I Tim. 2:15). I claimed this passage for myself and God assured me in my heart that he would deliver me from a painful childbirth. Around the 5th month, Paul preached about thinking positively. He used the illustration of the breaking out of the Bastille, a French prison which held various murderers, thieves and mental cases. On July 14th 1789, these prisoners made a successful escape out of the huge fortress... This was the date of the famous French Revolution Celebration. This holiday took on significance for me as a metaphor for my own 'breaking out' of mental bondage and illness, as well as for another very special reason which follows.

Less than a week later, Paul's Uncle, Cameron called. He casually mentioned that perhaps our baby would be born on July 14th, Bastille Day. Suddenly, Paul made the connection. Our baby would be born on that day to mark the miracle of my child's birth and my healing.

David Moss

David is a miracle to Paul and Me. We had put off having a family because of my mental health problems, having to be on medication to live a normal life. The doctor told me almost a year before that I was "making medical history" by overcoming my sickness. He was gradually taking me off my medicine. By January of '81 I was to be medicine free. Paul and I talked about having our first child soon after that. The lord had different plans. In September I started taking vitamin E for some small cysts I had and it threw off my system. I got pregnant in the middle of October. Paul and I were overjoyed! We danced round our living room when we found out the pregnancy test was positive. I called my doctor and he said that I could go off my medicine and would be just fine.

I had a very enjoyable pregnancy-felt great the whole time, kept my weight down (only gained 17lbs.), walked one hour everyday after jogging and ballet dancing until the 5th month. About the middle of the pregnancy the spirit reminded me of the scripture I Timothy 2:15:

"Notwithstanding she shall be saved in child bearing, if they continue in faith and charity and holiness with sobriety."

I claimed this passage and God assured me that he would deliver me from a painful childbirth.

Along bout the 5th month of my pregnancy Paul preached about thinking positively and used an illustration, the breaking out of the Bastille. The Bastille was a French prison in which various murderers, thieves, and mental cases were held. On July 14th, these prisoners made a successful escape from the huge fortress in which they were held. This date became known s Bastille Day or French Independence Day.

Less than a week later Paul's uncle Cameron called, he is a Presbyterian minister who lived in North Carolina. When asking bout the baby's due date, which was July 13th he casually mentioned that perhaps our child would be born on the 14th Bastille Day. Suddenly, Paul made the connection. Our baby would be born on July 14th to mark the miracle of my healing and our 1st child.

47

Tuesday July 14th, 1981 – Bastille Day

Blakely Time-3:30am-I woke up with the discomfort of early labor. After walking around bit, I realized that I was really going in to labor.

4:00am-I snuggled up to Paul and whispered, "Hey Paul, would you like to have our baby on Bastille Day?" Paul groggily responded, "Lets go back to sleep for awhile and make sure you're really ready to go to the hospital". Too excited to go back to sleep, I aroused Paul and we made preparations to drive to the hospital.

5:30am-We left for Flowers Hospital in Dothan, Alabama. I was so sick to my stomach and vomited a few times before getting into the car, and after that felt fairly comfortable. Paul calmly drove about 52 miles/hour, going easily over railroad tracks.

Alabama Time 6:00am-We are escorted through the emergency room and into the labor room.

6:45am-Dr. Gannon checked me before going off duty at 7:00am. "I think it might just be false labor." I replied, "I am sure that I'm going to have my baby today." "We'll see," he said as he turned to tell the nurse that I could have some breakfast. I drank a few gulps of apple juice but I lost it immediately. Meanwhile, Paul went to get a quick bite for himself.

8:00am-Dr. Flowers comes in, "you look too comfortable to be having a baby today. I'll be back at nine to check your progress.

9:15am-Dr. Flowers finds me 1cm dilated and 90% effaced, contractions coming regularly. He decides to break my water. "You'll have your baby sometime this evening." Until then I had been simply relaxing. At that point, I decided to begin the slow chest breathing I learned in Lamaze class.

11:30am-Since nothing to exciting was happening, Paul went to get a hamburger.

12:20pm-Dr. Flowers checked me again and discovered that I was 3cm dilated and 100% effaced. He ordered the nurse to add a few drops of Pitosin to my I.V. This sped up my labor. The contractions started coming every 2 minutes I remained calm by using the "hee" method. Only two times did I feel the impact of the contractions and Paul coached me to breathe "hee" louder.

1:15pm-I felt the urge to push and asked the nurse to examine me. Diane: "You couldn't have the urge to push yet!" "Please just check," I insisted. You should have seen her face when she found me 10cm dilated and felt the baby's head. "We've got to get you to the delivery room fast!" "Whatever you do don't push yet." The nurses scrambled, moving the big recliner out of the way, rolling the stretcher in for me. I felt so good that instead of edging my way onto the stretcher on my back, I did a complete flip. I gave the nurses a scare but it was easier that way. Diane threw Paul his scrub outfit and the pants fell to his ankles. We all laughed. I tried to hold back. We were off to the delivery room. When I looked back and the ticker tape that was pouring out of the machine which measures the pain level of contractions was filling the room, reminding me of my painless delivery.

1:30pm-Dr. Flowers arrives and quickly does an episiotomy. I only had to push 3 times and out cam our first born, our little miracle.

1:38pm-"It's a Boy!" I sang out in the excitement as the 1st Baptist Church bells chimed in the distance. What a blessing. Paul was snapping pictures during the whole event. The doctor was sewing me up as I leaned over to kiss my little David, the name that God told Paul to name our baby a couple of years before we were married. They laid me on my tummy which felt great after so many months they rolled me into my hospital room.

2:10pm-I couldn't quit telling my attending nurse Patricia all about the experience. God blessed me with the sweetest little Christian nurse. Paul bought me the hot fudge sundae he promised me earlier. I had a ravenous appetite; I could have eaten two suppers!

5:00pm-Paul and I walked around the maternity ward and beamed at David through the nursery windows. He had a full head of dark brown hair like Rocky.

It seems like a dream to me, it was so beautiful, after I had almost dismissed the thought of having a baby. The desire of my heart became a reality.

Psalm 37:4 states, "Delight thyself also in the Lord; and He shall give thee the desires of thine heart." When David was 5 ½ months old he suddenly said, 'I love you' and I was able to record it on tape. Few could understand how fully these words impacted us when they came from the mouth of our long awaited first child.

8

2 years old
David was looking at the pictures in a book on Missouri. He pointed to a waterfall and asked "what's that? I said "a waterfall". He said, "I'm sorry".

In 1982 they moved us again, this time to a little town called Woodland in Georgia. We ministered in a nearby town beside our friend David and his wife Nancy. They were two happy years for the most part. We square danced every Monday night. Little David clogged on the sidelines. They had given us a generous amount of food when we moved in. But persecution set in as usual.

This time we had four churches to deal with and it was rough. Paul was preaching four sermons every Sunday. God held him up. I got him out jogging with me every morning. He was strong. I however pulled the cartilage completely off my vertebrae. I had bent over to pick up David who weighed 35-40 lbs. and that's when it happened. The congregation was not happy that I had to be in a brace for two months and I would be six months healing. When we had to move from there to Hagan I was thankful for the help in packing.

In Claxton I enrolled David in preschool. I took a job selling Aloette products to supplement our income. Paul contracted a skin rash (all over body itch), that wouldn't go away. It proved to be the result of an internal condition. Anyway, during the services Paul was preaching hard against adultery. Then he was itching like crazy and not sleeping nights. In December of 1984 his mother called to say his father had passed. In January of the following year my husband of 12 years was diagnosed with terminal cancer.

They did surgery, and could not help him so the doctor gave him 6 months to live. He had lymphoma and it started in his pancreas. A tumor the size of a grapefruit was leaning on the duct and blocking it causing salt to build up. So the salt blockage was making him itch internally. Between Paul's mother and myself, we held vigil by his hospital bed and I walked the halls praying for him. I believed God had a plan.

That miracle came within several weeks. God took the tumor completely away. The all over body itch stopped and the scars from radiation treatments were healed. Paul was a new man. All of his treatment had taken place in Savannah. We loved being there. Our favorite ice cream shop was there even if Paul couldn't keep it down on the way home from radiation treatments. We incorporated our ministry there and made it a non-profit organization. Paul named it "Brother's Keepers" from the scripture in Genesis 4:9. We wanted to feed the poor out of our church but the members voted it down. Our district superintendent moved Paul to Albany, Ga. his hometown, so that in June we would have the support of his mom. Paul was given one church to care for. We had no clue what was coming ahead.

The parsonage had been abused by the previous couple. Among other things there was a roach infestation and there were metal objects in the lawn. Because of the state of our living quarters, we were really in need of encouragement. What we got was quite the opposite.

We found out Paul's cancer had returned. A congregation wants a healthy pastor and we believed this was the basis for some of the people to begin to play practical jokes on my husband. Someone would come into his office and mess up Sunday's bulletin. Later we found that our phone was tapped and the house was bugged. We had no privacy. As many as seven parishioners had keys to our parsonage, we found out. Paul thought I was doing these things partly because he didn't think churches would do such a thing, but this was part of the paranoia that had begun to set in, bringing him to the point of a nervous breakdown. He was losing sleep as well. Paul and I, and his mother discussed applying for disability. This was our 12th year of ministry together. By the end of 1985, he would have to end his public ministry.

Losing his ministry was one of the hardest things in the world for Paul, as it would be for anyone coming to the end of a hard won career. He loved to preach and teach the people, leading them to Jesus Christ. Visitation, a fast disappearing part of the pastoral ministry, was one of Paul's joys.

Eventually, my husband began to yell at me and take out his frustrations on those closest to him. Then the yells turned into curses. Why? I believe he was confused, between the cancer returning and the side effects of the medications, and I couldn't help him anymore.

Paul and his mother were making the trips to M.D. Anderson Hospital in Houston, Texas for chemotherapy. My mom graciously came to stay with David after he came home from the hospital where he was treated for bronchial pneumonia so that I could go to Texas to join Paul and his mom. He was not thriving there. It was a depressing atmosphere with thousands of patients pouring in daily. I did what I could and would change his catheter as I was taught in order to make sure nothing happened to his heart. Paul still vented his anger on me. One day I was changing his catheter for him and he got scared that I would make a mistake. He threw a mirror across the room. I just stood there, surprised. I had washed his feet and cared for him in his weakness. He just wasn't himself. I stayed for 10 days before returning home to our son David.

When Christmas came I bought David a kitten. He named him Striper for obvious reasons. Our Christmas tree was beautiful, but the kitten climbed on it knocking the ornaments to pieces on the ground. Then the kitten fell from a high tree, almost dying.

Paul was a very handsome man. A nurse's aide named Joanne began to set her sights on him. She informed me later of her strong attraction. I recalled too, that my father-in-law was not as close to Paul as his mother with whom my husband had a very close relationship. Many times 'Paw Paw' had said to me, "Barbara, there is no closer relationship in the entire world than Paul and his mom. I feel sorry for you." In the spring of 1987 he moved in with his mom because he claimed he could sleep better there. He told me to get David and me a place to live. So I did. I rented a little apartment five blocks away and I started looking for a job. I couldn't find anything that would pay enough. The only job I could find was teaching history part time for $90 per week. We couldn't make it on so little. I wasn't allowed to call Paul's mother because of her weak heart and when my husband picked up David for outings I had no contact. Our marriage was falling apart and Paul was out of line. While shopping for groceries I would burst into tears. One day Paul had a prophecy for me. "My daughter, your hands will paint again and your feet will dance again." What an encouragement to me! Then I was at a Bible study and had a vision of God's hand sweeping down and taking my hand and transporting me to another place. God was showing me and guiding me very strongly about the future. He had us covered!

Then the reverend of the First Methodist Church in Albany called me. He asked me to come to his office right away. He was serious and to the point. He was a man of experience and I listened to him. He said, "Barbara, does Paul have any firearms?" I said no and then he said, "Barbara we fear for your life." He had somehow heard of Paul's anger. Did he know my husband had thrown dishes at me? One plate got so close I could feel it pass my face. My life was in danger as things had spiraled out of control over the last 8 months. I began having nightmares that I was being shot. A friend came over at three in the morning and warned me it was time to leave. I truly didn't want to. Paul and his mother and I had been close for many years.

I was forced to call a lawyer and found the best in Albany. He said I would have to file for separation in order to gain custody of David. I told God that I didn't want to take Paul's son away from him, but it turned out to be the best decision for David's future. It was very painful for me when they served Paul the papers.

The playground at David's school was full of children and his first grade teacher was on duty. I walked up to David, got permission from the teacher, took my son's hand and walked slowly off the playground. As I was walking toward our 1977 Chevette I turned around and Paul was seconds behind me, talking to David's teacher. I turned back around, and the adrenaline flowing, knew that if I turned again I would give in and lose the composure I desperately needed as well as lose custody of David. I led my son to the car and told him to get in. He never saw his daddy. I pulled away and it was over.

Later God showed me there are three kinds of love, phileo (Gk.), or brotherly love, between a biological or spiritual brother or sister, eros (Gk.), or sexual love for a marital partner, and agape or unconditional love. Only God can give us this kind of love and it is eternal. Four aspects of this kind of love are commitment, faithfulness, communication and intimacy. In heaven we will be like the angels and sex will not be necessary.

I had to readjust my priorities to putting myself first, David second, and Paul third. I realized that I had always put God first, Paul second, David third, and me last. Life teaches us as we go along. For example, my mother believed that men were higher than women. She wasn't just submissive to my father, but passive too. His anger was so great that she was probably afraid and didn't do anything about the abuse. My brothers and sisters suffered for it. Dad knew nothing about building self-esteem in his children. Sadly, this story may have been different if he had had some medical help or counseling.

God taught me what I call **'The Five L's'** *Loving, Learning, Leaning, Losing and Letting Go*. If I had not let go of Paul and given him space there would have been a total catastrophe in my opinion. I didn't know what was going on behind the scenes. I just know that I couldn't stay in Albany. Paul and I had looked into living at a Christian community in Augusta, Ga. But it didn't work out.

God commanded me to forget the past so that he

could heal me. The only way I would make it without Paul was to have a strong support group. I made the arrangements with my parents for David and I to come to St. Louis. They had a big home and graciously gave us the okay.

9

25 months old
I had put David to bed when he called me back to his bedroom to
tell me, "I'm so happy momma".

God's will gradually unfolded for Paul, David and me. My separation from Paul was like trying to pull wallpaper off the wall because we had spent every waking hour together ministering side by side. I had to allow myself time to grieve. I would take long walks and cry so David wouldn't see me. There was a little park down the street where I poured my heart out to God. Our friends in Georgia had suggested that I look into Vineyard Fellowship as a church home, so I did.

For a little while David and I worshiped at Victory Fellowship, near my mom and dad's house until I got my own car. But once a week on Thursday night I would drive to 'Kinship', a Vineyard Fellowship group home for singles. The more I went to it, the more I realized that I was in the right place. Vineyard had the best worship singing in the nation, all the charismatic gifts operated in the congregation and there was a strong emphasis on healing and Bible teaching. Soon after I began going to the group, a young lady had a very encouraging statement for me, which she delivered (spoke) to me by the power of the Holy Spirit, as she operated in the charismatic gift of utterances as taught in the Bible. She said "Barbara kneel before me and put your head in my lap and I will heal you. I have a special place that I have prepared for you and I will lead you there." According to the Bible, as well, when a person receives such an encouraging message it will be repeated, or 'confirmed' by another source, being stated thus, 'let every word be confirmed in the mouth of two or more witnesses as a witness to the prophecy". A few months later a minister came to our cell group and asked, "Are you Barbara? God told me to tell you that after he finished healing the hurt he would use you in power and in might for His (Jesus') kingdom."

My healing was gradual. Right after my separation from Paul, my heart hurt so badly that I felt like I was having a heart attack. What saved me was pouring out to God my grief at the back of the church where the pastor, Randy Clark, let me dance. The worship lasted about 45 minutes and I benefited from that time so much. God was good to give David and me. We had good friends in the neighborhood too.

One day I was taking a walk on Briarton Dr. and as I got to one house the Lord told me to meet the owners. So I knocked on the door. A man named Rodger came to the door and I talked to him about my husband's cancer and he shared about his losing his first wife with cancer, then his current wife Pat came home and she said that her first husband had also died of cancer. We hit it off right away and they became close friends and supportive of me during that difficult time in my life and even to this day. At one point Pat was praying for her mother's house that had been up for sale for over one year. She told God that if he could help her sell her mother's home that she would give me $1000.00 for help to publish my book. The house sold within hours and the buyers paid cash for it. With good friends, mom and dad and David's good teachers, I was able to get emotionally stable again. I also went to dental assistant school and got a few part-time jobs which helped to rebuild my self-confidence.

I seek God early; some call it womb of the morning. Truly David was raised on praise. My times of worship in the park became deeper and longer. I leaned on God and knew His presence more and more. I wanted so badly to help my older brother Bob to be able to worship and perhaps snap out of his depression. We would go out every Friday night and visit at Schnuck's grocery in Webster Groves where we were raised and just talk. Mostly I would listen to him pour out his heart and pain. Then one day out of the blue, Bob said he would never talk to me again. I believe he was upset over the situation with Paul, which I did not feel I could fully reveal to him. Anyway, one day my brother and friend took his own life at age 45. It was February of 1989. He took an overdose and we got a call to come get him. He died on our front steps. As I held him in my arms in our living room, dad was still standing at the front door, just shaking his head, while mom was keeping David in the kitchen. How could I have prevented such a tragedy?

The funeral was tough. The burial was horrible. My two brothers and sister are buried side by side with only 'brother', 'brother' and 'sister' on their tombstones. My life would never be the same. Paul came up from Georgia, all right. He didn't have the courage to tell me in person who he brought with him so he gave David a letter to give me. He said that he brought a friend with him and they were going to get married. He didn't want to hurt me but he could not face cancer alone. Being away from David wasn't a good thing. Everyone seemed to want me to prevent visitation but I never once wanted to keep Paul from his only son.

God reassured me with the scriptures, Isa. 54 vs. 5-17 Israel, the restored "wife" of the Lord.

"For thy maker is thine husband. The lord of hosts is his name: and thy redeemer of the Holy one of Israel. The God of the whole earth shall be called. For the lord hath called thee as a woman forsaken and grieved in spirit, and a wife of youth, when thou was refused, saith thy God. For a moment have I forsaken thee, but with great mercies will I gather thee. In a little wrath I hid my face from thee for a moment: but with everlasting kindness will I have mercy on thee, saith the lord thy Redeemer.

For this is as the waters of Noah unto me: for as I have sworn that the waters of Noah should no more go over the earth; so have I sworn that I would not wrath with thee. For the mountains shall depart, and the hills be removed; but my kindness shall not depart from thee, neither shall the covenant of my peace be removed, saith the lord that hath mercy on thee.

O thou afflicted, tossed with tempest, and not comforted, behold, I will lay thy stones with fair colors, and lay thy foundations with sapphires. And I will make thy windows of agates, and thy gates of carbuncles, and all thy borders of pleasant stones.

And all thy children shall be taught of the Lord; and great shall be the peace of thy children. In righteousness shalt thou be established: thou shalt be far from oppression; for thou shalt not fear: and from terror; for it shall not come near thee. Behold they shall surely gather together against thee shall fall for thy sake.

Behold I have created the smith that bloweth the coals in the fire, and that bringeth forth an instrument for his work; and I have created the waster to destroy. No weapon that is formed against thee shall prosper; and every tongue that shall rise against thee in judgment thou shalt condemn. This is the heritage of the servants of the lord, and their righteousness is of me, saith the Lord."

10

26 months
David was eating bread on the sofa, and he stuck his fingers into
the bread making a nice round HOLE. He showed me and said
"momma, I'm going to eat the WHOLE thing."

Paul and Joanne wanted me to file for divorce but I
didn't. I don't believe in divorce. It isn't God's will. God
gave the Israelites permission to put away their wives only
because Moses pleaded with God to have mercy. God said
only because of the hardness of their hearts would he allow
it. So Paul filed for divorce. They had lived together since
March of 1989 anyway so why not make it lawful? The
divorce date was set for December 7, 1989, Pearl Harbor
day.

I'm sure Paul explained it to David because of the
good father that he was. I remember walking into the
courthouse in somewhat of a daze. Having to lose Paul was
not possible for me without God's help. I was early as usual
and after having looked around for Paul, decided to ask
someone where our case would be in session. I walked into
the room and took my seat on the right side. Soon Paul and
Joanne appeared on the left side and sat down. The judge
called me to the front and I took the stand. I was in
complete composure knowing that custody of David would
go to me. Paul and Joanne actually looked good together,
Paul with his graying beard and her being nicely dressed
and 14 years older, I had no choice but to trust God. On the
way home I reflected upon years gone by and felt a peace

that passes all understanding. Paul and Joanne got married on January 28, 1990, exactly 5 years after Paul was diagnosed with lymphoma, a deadly cancer. Paul and his mom and dad shared the same anniversary. I remembered what Joanne had told me that God had told her, "You will marry a minister in 5 years." A door in my life had closed and my faithful God was opening another one.

David and I moved to Jefferson Barracks apartments where I raised David the rest of the way through high school. The rent was affordable. I chose it because: Mehlville was a good school district, it was near our church, Vineyard Fellowship, and Sylvan Springs Park was a lovely place to enjoy. God provided and protected David and me in so many ways the whole time I was a single mom and dealing with Bi-Polar I Disorder.

The Lord was giving me a sign of provision. When I found a dime and a penny on the ground or floor it meant that he was taking care of our financial needs. One Sunday morning we were in church and David had to go to the bathroom. He came running into the back of the church crying, "Mommy, mommy, there's a dime and a penny in the toilet!" Another way God provided was the way visitation was going. We were sharing David so nicely. David was playing on a baseball team. Paul was driving back and forth to pick up our son and I would get to visit with him a little while. Paul provided nice clothes for David as a form of child support. The Sylvan Springs Park gave me a perfect place to worship and praise God. Every morning I would get up at the crack of dawn and go to the park and sing, and then I would come home and get David up, fix him breakfast and see David off to the school bus, usually with perfect timing. One morning I was walking to the pavilion and I saw a picture in my mind of a man shabbily dressed sleeping on a picnic table. All of a sudden there was a feeling of evil all around me, gripping me. When I approached the place where I worshipped there was a man dressed in poor rags sleeping on the picnic bench. I very carefully backed up and went the other way. God had warned me of danger. I normally would have talked to him without fear but not that day, thanks to the Lord my protector. I would have been harmed trying to bring him to Christ.

One way I restored my soul was by bringing songs that Paul and I used to sing together then changing words toward adoration of the Lord Jesus. For example: "Oh My Dove," from Song of Solomon in the Bible. "You Needed Me," Paul's and my theme song. I would also sing "A Time For Us," and "You'll Never Walk Alone."

The words to one song called "Miracles" are very touching. "Miracles, miracles, people say don't be mystic. Miracles, miracles, dawn to dusk a way of life. Miracles, miracles come on girl be realistic. My own eyes see. My own hands feel. I know this miracle's for real. I know this miracle's for real." I would sing songs over and over again until a peace fell on me then I would intercede for my family, church, the nation and the whole world. After doing this for about 7 years, one morning I noticed a man on a hill nearby with arms outstretched to heaven praising God and then on the other side of me another man was worshipping God with his arms straight up. What a blessing! It helps me to be out in nature to worship the King of the Universe. One time, two baby fawns were playing on the hill beside me. There were always woodchucks and birds, of course, squirrels everywhere. Sometimes, I felt like St. Francis of Assisi because of all of the nature around me.

One beautiful morning I got caught up in worship and lost track of time. It must have been on a weekend because I wasn't late for work. I looked at my watch and I had been in the park for 2 ½ hours! I decided to take the long road home by Jefferson Barracks Cemetery. I paused to look at all of the graves, about 170,000 at that time! All of a sudden I had an open vision, which means that my eyes were wide open. I saw all the graves open up and the spirits of the people rising up out of the graves. They moved up and then dissipated. The vision only lasted a few seconds. I just stood there in awe. I thought, "What is God trying to tell me?" Perhaps I would live to see the second coming of Jesus Christ? I didn't tell very many people about what I saw.

11

29 months old
David looked down at his feet and said "momma, I'm going to
outgrow my toes."

Paul and I had some touching times before his cancer
returned. He would come to pick David up after school, but
come a little early so we had time together. About that time
we took a walk and his honesty was too much. He started
to tell me how good his intimate times with Joanne were. I
remember having mixed feelings. I was happy for him but
changed the subject as tears started coming to my eyes.
"Let's go home, David's probably getting off the school bus
soon," I said. We walked home in silence. The joy of seeing
Paul and David together was enough to uplift me. Paul
knew how much I still loved him but he was always honest
with me. He said "the reason I was so bad to you is because
I was jealous of you." First of all, you're selfless and second
you're too industrious and you minister better than I do.
Plus you get to raise David and I don't." He knew me so
well and I knew his thoughts almost all of the time. Were
we too close? One afternoon Paul came to ask me to help
him. He told me that Joanne had a severe headache and she
needed me. I naturally dropped everything and got in the
station wagon with him. Before we got down the street
Paul said, "Barbara, sing to me." I started singing one song
after the other and sang almost the whole way to St. Peters.
About half way there Paul looked at me and reached over

to take my hand. I let him gently hold my hand. Tears seemed to be forming in the corners of his eyes. I also held back tears. We pulled up into the driveway of their trailer and Paul escorted me in. Joanne was in the bedroom. We went in and I could tell they had a disagreement or marital spat of some kind. No questions asked I dropped to my knees and prayed for Joanne first and then Paul and begged the Lord to heal and strengthen them. I knew how much Paul needed Joanne and so I was able to hold my emotions together. I got back to my feet and Paul led me into the kitchen. Face to face he put his hands under my elbows and looked me square in the eyes saying, "I want both of you." Joanne slipped quietly into the dining room, and led me out to the car. She hadn't said a word the whole evening. The 45 minute drive with Joanne seemed long because of the total silence. Joanne treated me with more respect after that landmark day. Previously she would write letters to me telling me to commit suicide so they could get custody of David.

12

Paw Paw said, "Now we have a son to carry the Moss name"!
David piped up and said "You carry it"!

Vineyard was such a wonderful church for
fellowship and yet I was not growing for some reason. One
Sunday a woman came up to me. She said that I was in a
box and needed to break free. She asked me if I wanted to
come to her apartment after church and I said "yes". It was
right beside the church so we walked over. She was a
counselor and a prophetess. God sent her to me for a very
important reason. I was stuck and couldn't go forward. She
prophesied over me on April 14, 1993.

> "Think not my daughter that you have come this
> way for naught. Spring is upon the earth. My words
> are springing forth. Your song you've been singing
> about April is true. It's time for blossoming. Your
> faithfulness is great, Oh, my daughter. I hold you in
> the hollow of my hand. Many have tried to snatch
> you out of my hand I say they are removed.
> Daughter, I have separated you, I have prepared
> you, your birth is like new spring, and freshness is at
> the door. Fear not for as I promised to be with
> Joshua and Esther, I will never leave you. Go forth
> boldly speaking the truth in love.

I have tried you. You have been obedient to the servant under which I have placed you. Walk in newness of revelation knowledge. Walk not in the past. Take my hand come afresh. Be open to the gifts that I will bring. You are my special one. You have been a foot soldier. Hold fast to what you have heard this day. I want you walking in my Spirit. Be a God pleaser, sayeth the Lord Almighty."

Vineyard Fellowship had been such a wonderful place for David and me to be. The worship music kept getting better all the time. Pastor Randy was more fired up as he grew and matured. We were ministering at the projects in downtown St. Louis. Our cell group was closely knit and we had fun together: picnics and volleyball were my favorites. I prayed about a possible new church and the next day I was introduced to Trinity church. There was a strong women's' group and they were studying a workbook on codependency. It was perfect for me! They had a nice youth group for David too. So we transferred our membership to Trinity.

The first Sunday in May of 1994 I got a phone call that Paul's kidneys had failed and that he was dying. I went to the 8:00 service in the chapel at my new church. Just outside I began to cry out to God in grief, "Please do something, and help me!" I went into the service and sat down in the back. There was a guest minister there that morning, a prophet from Tulsa. Immediately he said, "Young lady," looking straight at me, "come up here." He then prophesied over me saying, "My daughter, this day your ministry is birthed. All you have to do is go home and pray." Then he laid his hands on me and I was overwhelmed by the Holy Spirit. I went home and prayed in the Spirit for a very long time and a peace fell over me that kept me through the emotionally difficult week ahead.

Memaw, Paul's mom, and Carol, his sister came up from Georgia. I fed them a meal of pot roast and blessed them and we had fellowship time. They got to see Paul before he died on May 5th at 2:00 in the morning. I was not allowed to go to Paul's funeral because Joanne threatened me. So David at age 12 went with Memaw and Carol. I loved Paul so much. He was my one and only. It was extremely difficult for me to stay home. He was buried in Albany, GA, his home town. Later David told me that they played Paul singing El Shadi on cassette tape at his funeral. He had such a beautiful voice.

13

Christmas 1983
2 ½ years old
David said, "I can't find my OTHER
stocking.

With Paul gone it was much easier for me to
concentrate on my ministry. I remember feeling so relieved
and glad that he wasn't suffering in any way. Even better
he was blessed in heaven by his Heavenly father. The small
group I led at church was going very well and helping me
to understand myself better too. At church one morning I
was up front for an altar call. We were all gathered around
and asked to pray for a lady with severe pain in her right
side. The minute I touched her, the power of God hit me
from above like a bolt of lightning. I would have fallen
completely to the floor if I had not glanced to the side and
grabbed the forearm of a man standing to the right of me.
Pastor Joel was watching me and when I got back up asked
me, "What can I do for you?" I said that the gift of healing
was flowing. He said, "I'll say!" and turned to grab the
anointing oil from the altar, splashed it on both of my
hands, put them together, held them between his hands
and prayed, "God bless the gift you have given her." Soon
after that happened, one of Pastor Joel's elders, Wally,
invited me to be a part of the Trinity Ministerial

Association Fellowship. Soon after that they gave me the opportunity to be an altar minister. God was rewarding me for putting him first in my life and because of the time of worship I spent with him every morning. My ministry was beginning to take off.

The sleep trouble I had for so many years, common to the manic side of me, was really getting to me. One night in August I told God that I was angry and felt like throwing my bed out of the window. A few weeks later God answered my plea. It was August 28, 1994. We had just finished having our nightly prayers. I said goodnight to my son and was lying face up on my bed meditating. Suddenly, the glory of God came and entered into my bedroom in the form of a bright white light, which flooded my entire room. I was awe-struck and laid there glued to my bed. The presence of the Holy Spirit slowly moved across my entire body beginning with my feet, moving upward then resting on my left hand. My hand began to dance without me doing it. Bright light like laser beams shot out of my hand. Then God's healing touch rested on my head. After about 2 minutes the light of God's glory slowly faded and I went right to sleep in total peace. I began sleeping well every night. It was a miracle just like I was on the operating table of God!

Our church was moving together quickly now. We now called ourselves the "Hospital Church." There were so many of us that were called by God to minister in some way. It was difficult, I'm sure, to keep the congregation united. This scripture jumped off the page one day when I was reading my bible.

> *"Now glory be to God who by his mighty power at work within us is able to do far more than we would ever dare to ask or even desire or dream of-infinitely beyond our highest prayers, desires, thoughts or hopes. May he be given glory forever and ever throughout endless ages because of his master plan of salvation for the church through Jesus Christ."* Ephs.3:20-21

My son David was doing well at this time. He was active in the church youth group and played the guitar on the worship team. Walt at our church had given him a prophecy about two months before his father died. "David, you have had angels all around you protecting you. Now I am removing the one from behind you because you have no need of him. You will never have to walk that path again. You will move forward from now on." He seemed to be flourishing in every area of his life and I was proud of him for overcoming so much.

Doris the leader of the women at the Trinity church invited me to be one of the speakers at the fall retreat. So on Oct. 13th 1995 I stood before the ladies of the church and gave my testimony. The themes running through my message were forgiveness and gratitude. We are responsible to walk in love. I had to forgive my father for his anger and then my husband Paul too. By God's grace I had the victory. A humble man cannot be provoked to anger. Towards the end I shared my gratefulness for getting to be married and having my son David and the promise of my ministry. I closed with this little but profound story.

"I had a tiny box, a precious box, of human love-my spikenard (aromatic oil or root) of great price. I kept it close within my heart of hearts

"And scare would lift the lid lest it should waste its perfume on the air

"One day a strange deep sorrow came with crushing weight and fell upon my costly treasure; sweet and rare and broke the box to atoms!

"All my heart rose in dismay and sorrow at this waste.

"But as I mourned, behold a miracle of grace Divine! My human love was changed to Heavens Own, and poured in healing steams on other broken hearts,

While soft and clear, a voice above me whispered, "Child of Mine, with comfort wherewith thou art comforted, from this time forth, go comfort others."

"And thou shalt know blest fellowship with Me, Whose broken heart of love hath healed the world."

As soon as those words left my lips, there was a standing ovation. Pastor Sherri was beaming, Carla was excited and Doris looked so proud. God had turned Friday the 13th into a great day for us all!

The Lord had helped me use my areas of strength in providing work for me. At one time, I had three different employers, St. John's Mercy Hospital and two other home health agencies. Once someone asked me where I worked

and I said "St. John's Mercy, etc. mercy, mercy, mercy."
Then we laughed. When juggling three jobs got to be too
much I found out that I could be a substitute teacher with
my Oklahoma teacher's certificate. So I went for an
interview.

The day was a beautiful one and I felt confident in
my spirit that they would accept me for employment. The
interview went well but for some reason they turned me
down. I walked out feeling defeated and not knowing what
to do next. When I was half way to my car, a lady came
running out of the door. She yelled across the parking lot,
"Wait a minute, wait a minute, come back!" They had
looked at my college transcript and reconsidered. I got the
job! My new work covered students of all ages and needs:
physical, emotional, and behavioral. My job with the
Special School District was challenging and drew on my
compassion. God gave me the perfect hours to take care of
David as a single mom. I got home about the same time as
he did.

14

After seeing Santa at the Columbus mall,
David exclaimed, "Santa has sharp knees".

During our years at Jefferson apartments, God gave me a friend that was so in tune with God about my situation. One day she had just awakened from a nap and she'd had a dream. At the end of the dream, God told her to tell me right away. I came to her house just as she finished the dream. She looked stunned when she came to the door. She was still in awe and anointed by the Holy Spirit. In the dream I was walking toward her. There was a big white light behind me. I asked her "where do I go?" She sensed that I needed to walk toward the light and that God had a ministry just for me near my home. God wanted to hold me and take care of me. That I must lead out, and then others would follow. Soon after that I jumped into my car and started driving toward St. Louis on Telegraph Road. God led me to a poor neighborhood off of Broadway. My ministry was to the poor, sick and African-Americans. As I turned onto a little side street I discovered a pasture with real live sheep right there in the city! I would go there first thing in the morning and pray. Often tears would come to my eyes in thanksgiving for all of God's blessings. Then I would go door to door as the Holy Spirit led me. If I got a check in my spirit I would not go to the house but I covered most of the homes in the blocks around Notre Dame School. After about two years I called the evangelism style "friendship evangelism" because I would establish a relationship with the people before I even shared Jesus Christ with them. I came across many interesting situations.

One particular household that was very responsive to me told me that God protected me from going to some of the houses because evil had lurked there. One family in the community was known for their meanness and some were on drugs. A positive experience was when I came to the door of one of my special education students. His family so graciously escorted me into their home time and time again. Another time I came to the door of a young woman that had just lost her three-year old son by drowning in their own swimming pool! She was a Methodist as I had been. So I was able to comfort her. She received well. Time and time again I was able to help someone, pray for them and intercede for their family. Psalms 35:10 says,

> *"all my bones shall say, Lord who is like unto thee, which deliverest the poor from him that is too strong for him, hey, the poor and the needy from him that spoileth him?*

One of my fondest memories was of an elderly woman named Gertrude. She lived with an older man. They weren't married but she was 97 and he looked out for her as best he could. Then for some odd reason he became abusive. When I found out and told her cousin David and I prayed for her safety. A neighbor ended up intervening and the elderly man went to his folks up north. David and I decided to put Gertrude in a nursing home. He said to me, "You're a minister, aren't you?" I told him that God had ordained me but not a man. I took Gertrude communion and loved her till she died several months later at age 98.

I did face persecution during this time. One of my neighbors who disliked me for my stand for Jesus uprooted my flower garden. I planted some more flowers but she did it again. I was more concerned about her than my flowers. Her heart finally softened then she moved.

I lost my job after being ill-treated at a junior high school. I taught many different types of children some having mild to severe cases of Down syndrome, spinal bifida, behavioral and autistic disorders. This provided me a great challenge. A teacher across the hall took my substitute folder before I got to class one morning. So I had to wing it alone all day not knowing what I was supposed to be teaching on. Then I was put in an all behavioral disorder, all boys' class at Mehville High school. The boys were so horrible that I had tears running down and I wanted to leave so bad. They had the foulest mouths you could imagine in three different categories: bathroom talk, sexual filth, and cursed God. They did everything they could to drive me crazy. When the bell rang at 3:30 I just about crawled out of the room and knew that I would never come back. They should have put a football coach in that classroom!

The persecution escalated to also include my church. Some of the women were coming to my house for prayer and fellowship. The church leadership discouraged this. I think they wanted to keep everything at church. Words were said from the pastor and I just had to leave. I walked out, scraped the dust off my sandals and never returned. God took care of the situation and I went back to my old church, Vineyard Fellowship. I started a bible study in my home and a lady named Donna was the facilitator. A friend played the guitar and we had some people from the apartment complex come. One young lady gave her life to Jesus.

A few weeks later I got a letter from the Special School District asking for my resignation from my teaching job. They said that I was too kind. With a sigh of relief, I began looking for another job. I interviewed at the YMCA and surprisingly they offered me a job at St. Bernadette's

Catholic School right by our apartment complex! I worked the after school care for the Latchkey program. It was perfect for me to take care of David too. He was a teenager then and I had to be available to him. God encouraged me with these words from the book of Zeph 3:16-20

> *"Cheer up don't be afraid, for the Lord your God has arrived to live among you. He is a mighty Savior. He will give you victory. He will rejoice over you in great gladness, he will love you and not accuse you. I have gathered your wounds and have taken away your reproach. I will deal severely with all those who have oppressed you. I will save the weak and helpless. I will gather you and give you a good name of distinction among your people and restore your fortunes before their eyes."*

About this time of reflecting I was taking a nap and woke up looking at my clock. There was an aura of purple light surrounding it and radiating out of it. Then as I glanced up to look out the window I realized that the whole sky was a gorgeous purple. God told me that he had everything under control. I was comforted and ready to go on.

15

January 1984
David, "I dreamed about Jesus.
He's writing a book. 'Paul' is your name in the book." David said,
"Not yet".

In Augusta, GA the place where we looked into living, there was witchcraft. It was known as a Christian Community. But where Jesus works, Satan comes up with a strong counter-attack. The Devil undermines everything we as Christians try to do. The bible says in John 10:10 that "*the devil is out to steal, kill and destroy.*"

When David was in High School, there was a boy on the school bus who was into witchcraft. David told me about him and I went to his house to investigate. His mom answered the door and welcomed me in. I talked to her for a while just as a neighbor and she was very pleasant. Then her son came up from the basement. As I talked with him I sensed some peculiar speech. I got up and walked to the basement door and he said something like "you don't want to go down there" and so I didn't. He was a little creepy. I didn't want to stay any longer and so I left. Years later my suspicions were found to be true. At the bottom of the steps to Sylvan Springs Park I had an encounter that I will never forget. A boy about eleven years old was coming down the steps and I met him coming up. We fell into conversation. All of a sudden his voice changed and he was speaking evil words. A demon had taken over. I stood firm and spoke of the love of God and how much Jesus loved him. After several minutes his voice came to a turning point. He spoke in his normal voice, pivoted about and walked back up the steps. I never saw him again but I did find out that he hung out with the boy who was into witchcraft on David's school bus.

The gift of discernment became another important aspect of my ministry. I was beginning to have experiences in the realm of the spirit. For instance, I was talking to a young man by the swimming pool in our apartment complex and all of a sudden a dark cloud came out of him and dissipated into the pool. God told me that he had the spirit of lust. Later I found him flirting with a woman almost 20 years older than him. One day as I was dancing at the back of Vineyard Fellowship I saw a black cloud coming out of a man in the congregation and it disappeared into the thin air. I didn't know him but the Lord showed me just as clear as can be to stay away from certain people. Also at this time I was finding great favor with God and man. At our cell group at Christy and Todd's home we were sitting around the kitchen table and there was a knock on the door. It was a minister from Illinois whom nobody knew. He said, "I need to speak to Barbara." I said, "I'm Barbara." He took me to the side of the room and opened his bible to Matt. 9:18 which tells me of a miracle where Jesus raises a young 12 year old girl from the dead. He looked deep into my eyes and said, "Barbara, you will be doing this too." Then he left. I stood there for a moment recalling the time that God raised a man from the dead during our ministry in Georgia. I was sitting on a pew and Paul was preaching when the elderly man beside me fell forward dead. A nurse in the congregation immediately came to check his pulse. I was praying in the Spirit. She said, "He's gone." I said, "No!" and continued praying. She kept her fingers on his wrist for nine long, seemingly endless minutes. I was determined not to give up on him. Paul was standing frozen in the pulpit. The congregation remained silent. Finally the man of eighty or so got up and sat down by me and Paul went on with his sermon as if nothing had happened.

In March of 1995, my sister called me about their dog, Shane. Shane was a beautiful Siberian husky. He was so sick that they were going to put him to sleep. I went out on Sunday afternoon to pray for Shane who had a tumor the size of a grapefruit behind his front leg. The vet had diagnosed cancer in his lungs and lymph nodes. When Sally called the vet to put the dog to sleep, he was out of town. But Tuesday the tumor had shrunk becoming concave instead of convex and was draining out a hole in the middle. Shane perked up and started playing with Blizzard, their other Siberian Husky as he was accustomed. Sally's faith was boosted and I was praising the Lord for the miracle. Shane lived about 4 years longer to about 14 years old.

At volleyball, an acquaintance of mine, Peggy, jammed her thumb very badly. She was crying out in pain and the ice pack wouldn't activate. She went outside and sat on the curb alone. I took the opportunity and asked her if I could pray for her. She immediately laid her thumb in my hand out of desperation. I prayed and she could move her thumb. We rejoiced and she got up and played volleyball, my favorite sport.

Lena, a friend of mine from church and I went to Barnes Hospital to pray for a 20 year old man who had leukemia. Pastor Joel gave us Joe's name to pray for too. We ended up praying for three people. The next day we found out that Joe's x-rays showed that God had healed his heart and all the scars from his heart attack. We glorified God together! I kept seeing light in my eyes every time I closed them and during the church services. Our church was so on fire that one morning I got drunk in the spirit and could barely walk straight. I wanted to dance but Pastor Joel wouldn't allow it. Then one day in the chapel Pastor Joel gave me permission to dance. Lena was sitting right by me. The music began and Pastor Joel waved his hand across the floor as he looked at me. I got up and danced to a song I had never heard and then sat down. Then we all worshipped the Lord by singing an Israeli song.

God was using me in ministry, as he always had, in spite of my battle with mental illness. One morning I was washing dishes and looked out the kitchen window. My neighbor was hobbling toward her apartment. I could tell that there was something wrong with her foot. All of a sudden liquid love came from Heaven and poured into my heart. Before I knew it my foot started carrying me out my front door and around my apartment to hers. I asked her what happened and she said that her foot was broken in two, completely severed! "Please let me pray for you," I said. She said yes and I took her hand and said a simple prayer of faith and then left. Again I was in my kitchen that afternoon and looked out my window. Low and behold she was completely healed. The doctor had x-rayed it a second time and found the bone to be perfectly knit together. He said, "I don't know what happened but you are all healed." She said, "I do. My neighbor prayed for me." After that mighty miracle she was so thankful to me that she cooked supper for David and me every Wednesday for several weeks. She was African-American and boy could she cook! Soon after that she moved away. She never told anybody about her foot.

When I was still at my apartment at Jefferson Barracks I was babysitting for my friend's daughter. She became out of hand, getting into everything and I noticed her eyes rolling back in her head. I laid my hands on her head and prayed, "Satan leave her alone in Jesus' name!" Immediately she became calm and docile and played peacefully. I told her mom the next day and she said that her behavior was unruly when she returned from her father's house after the weekend of visitation, for they were divorced. That poor child of about four years old was already influenced by the demonic. Her mom thanked me and much prayer went up for her daughter. Another time, a lady also in our apartment complex was deeply troubled and manifesting some demonic bondage. I prayed a simple prayer over her and she was set free. God was soon to show me the steps to leading someone out of bondage into his marvelous light!

16

3 years old
Tent camping for the first time-
David looks up at the ceiling of
our pup tent and says, "Could you please move this?"

When David turned 16 he sewed some wild oats. His hormones changed and he started going around with some friends at school that led him astray. He wasn't himself and it was hard for him not having a daddy. Also I had my hands full because he was 6 feet tall and 170 lbs. God helped me hold us together. One time David and his friend came into our living room demanding that I let David buy a 1995 Mitsubishi with the interest on his daddy's pension. I had already bought him a 1988 prelude when the school bus was not safe. His friend glared at me and threatened to kill me if I didn't buy the car for David. I should have called the police. Maybe that would have helped, but maybe not. I decided to get the black 1995 sports car for David. Although it was a mistake, I am thankful that God protected David.

As a result of my ministry and affiliation with others in ministry, I was invited to the first Oral Roberts Ministerial Conference in October 1998 held in Tulsa, Oklahoma. I flew there and a man from Oral Roberts University met me at the airport and took me to the hotel room. It was right across from the campus so I walked to and from the scheduled activities. Richard Roberts, Oral's son, spoke and a few other guest speakers. One meal time I was sharing my intercessory prayer times with a minister and something awesome and funny at the same time happened as I related to him my sincere, heartfelt desire to see the barriers between denominations come down. A partition between our table and the hallway fell down making a loud crashing noise. We both laughed and had to compose ourselves. This is a verse that God gave me on October 15, 1998 which applies to the ministerial conference: Jeremiah 6:16

"Thus saith the Lord, Stand ye in the ways, and see, for the old paths where is the good way, and walk therein, and ye shall find rest for your souls."

Rev. Billy Joe Daugherty, a good friend of Paul's admonished us saying, "Things that were aborted, abandoned or miscarried in the past will work this time for the Glory of God." About this fall season, God told me to, "Run to the cross and flee the resurrection!" (Be ready to sacrifice and not want glory). It was a wonderful experience and I came home full of the Holy Spirit and with more zeal to serve my master.

In his senior year, David's grades slipped and he didn't even care. He almost did not walk with his class because he was flunking psychology. At the last of the semester his teacher let him write a term paper so that he got a D in her class. When they called David's name during graduation I yelled out "Thank you Jesus" at the top of my lungs not caring what the people around me thought. That spring David and I drove to Springfield, MO to look at Drury University. We were both impressed with the campus. But God had some work to do in David before he was ready to go off to college.

When David was 18 years old he moved in with his friend. At the same time on his July birthday he lost support from the government, but he still had his daddy's pension from the United Methodist Church. I lost my job that summer also. Then my rent went up. I knew I couldn't pay my bills so I moved in with a friend from church. Right away I got a job in day care taking care of infants. I loved it and my boss loved me. The lady that I was sharing an apartment with was so happy, until something bad happened. We had been shopping together and she had sleep trouble that night so we went to our separate bedrooms and she was trying to sleep. I was quiet for over three hours then decided to go for a walk in Tower Grove Park. As I was walking across the kitchen floor the boards creaked and my shoes made some noise. Out from under the doorway my friend came flying out of her bedroom and plastered me against the wall by the bathroom door. She tried to choke me, and as I felt my breath being cut off I used all my strength to push her away. I managed to get away and ran out the front door.

In the fall of 1999 I found myself drinking more water than usual and crunching on ice. Plus I was waking up too early in the morning. One morning I had woken up too early and apparently had been washing my medicine out of my system by drinking way too much water. My roommate and I drove all over the place trying to find a ring for her. I found myself losing patience with her because I hadn't slept and was sick. I laid into her on the way home. She told me to pack my bags and leave and so I did. This was not like me at all! I should have gone straight to the doctor. My mom and dad were in California visiting my Uncle Frank and Aunt Nancy. I didn't know where to go. I went to the Villas where mom and dad lived and asked them if I could spend the night there. They were very accommodating and welcomed me with open arms. By this time I was going into a manic state. I walked over to Delmar Gardens, the nursing home right beside the Villas and was just wandering around by then. I talked to one of the staff there and then meandered back to the Villas. Thank God, the lady at Delmar Gardens called and told the staff at the retirement center that I had come by and wasn't making any sense. By then I had gone up to the apartment and I heard a knock at the door. It was the housekeeper. She was so compassionate, so sweet and so sensitive. We talked for a little while. I gained my composure. Then she left. I'm surprised they didn't at least suggest I go to the doctor. I managed to make it okay until my mom and dad got back from their vacation in California.

When mom and dad came home they were surprised to see me and could tell how sick I was. The rules were that guests were allowed to stay several nights to two weeks. My brother came over and was concerned about my causing them to lose their retirement apartment. I packed up and left. I didn't have the foggiest idea where to go, so I pulled in a friend's drive way and knocked on the door. Jeff answered and welcomed me in. He and his first wife had been good friends to me for several years. I knew that he had a new wife so I didn't want to bother them. Composing myself I made a request to sleep in my car in his driveway. He said "Yes, not a problem." It was October and the evenings were heavenly. The only problem is my car had bucket seats and the back seat had a lump in the middle. So the first night I hardly slept at all!! My 1991 Sunbird convertible wasn't made to be a hotel! The second night I requested to stay in Jeff's car and I managed to get some shuteye. I knew I couldn't go on like this. My sister Sally came to my rescue. Jeff must have called my family.

Sally called me to invite me to the Billy Graham Crusade. I was surprised and excited. Instead she took me to Deaconess Hospital. I remember it being very hard for her. They kept me three nights but I was okay so I called all over. Every homeless shelter was full and Reverend Larry Rice was at full occupancy. Finally I called a place in O'Fallon where I could stay for five nights. They were so good to me and I had a beautiful field to pray in. The Lord led me to call Ginny, Jeff's first wife who had remarried.

Ginny was so pleased to hear from me and she and her husband Joe welcomed me to stay with them for a while. Ginny was as sweet as she could be, cooking for me and fellowshipping. But I could only stay there one week since they needed their privacy. I decided to call my close friends Pat and Roger. They said that I could come and live with them as long as I needed. We had some happy times together but they were struggling financially and eventually were forced to file for bankruptcy. Their house was put up for sale on the courthouse steps. Thank God I was able to help them at this difficult time in their lives. I would pack their belongings up during the day while they were at work. They had a very successful estate sale. By then I was sleeping on their sofa in the living room with a TV set on the floor. There was nothing left in the house! Because I was still in contact with some of my sisters in Christ from my church, God was leading me into an experience of a lifetime.

For several months the Lord seemed to be leading me into missions again. A close Christian girlfriend had a vision of me in a circle with other people. I was leaning over creating something in my hands like pottery and she said that I was on an island. Two other friends had similar influences from the Spirit. I was watching TV one day and the island of Australia was being described. Perhaps it was a travelogue or something but I only saw a small portion of the program. Next, I went to the library to look into the country "down under." I did some research and began praying about whether I should go there.

Preparations started falling into place. God had given me $513.34 from my bank because of a mistake on the bank's part. Plus the police department had given me $100 for appreciation for my ministry in the poor neighborhood. I still had some extra money in my bank account that I kept for when I returned to the USA. I sold several of my watercolor paintings and bought a plane ticket. The travel agent went overboard helping me when he found out my reason for going. When I wrote out my check it was number 777 which is a sign because 7 is considered the perfect number. My friend, Jan, knew a missionary family in Australia that she arranged for me to stay with. I got medicine from my doctor to be prepared for any situation that might come up while I was gone from the states. David was staying with a friend and his father. So I felt like I had the green light to search for God's will for my life.

Thanksgiving day my dear son, David, at age 18, picked me up and took me to the St. Louis airport. He was so mature, so special and difficult to leave. He understood my heart to minister wherever God called me. He was to start Meramec Community College in January of 2000 and had a part time job. He wasn't where I had hoped he would be spiritually, but I knew all I could do was to pray. What better place to pray than the other side of the world, where I couldn't see the circumstances and worry. My plane left

St. Louis on time and landed in Los Angeles where we had a brief layover. My plane was a 747 Quantas and we left from Los Angeles at 10:30 pm on November 24. I enjoyed Thanksgiving in the air. I felt close to God as I looked down on the vast ocean. We arrived in Sydney Australia at 8:00 am on Friday November 26 because we had crossed the dateline.

I called a nearby church and they graciously took me to the youth hostel. I stayed at the hostel 4 days and ate at Market city, near China Town. I experienced being among 65% Orientals for those 4 days. It was fascinating and educational. My pursuit for learning about the Aborigines was intensified when I found out that they had been mistreated and put in projects.

In Sydney I checked into a boarding house with my many pieces of luggage, how I managed them God only knows. At the same time a group of men from Germany arrived. We had a lot of fun singing and laughing. One of them played the guitar and was very talented. They were not Christians so I witnessed to them the love of God for them. The only problem is that I found myself going into a manic state. I took a walk for hours all over Sydney and it started raining. By the time I got back to the boarding house I was in an "altered" state, (manic- with irrational thinking, increased vulnerability). The person at the desk called the police and they came and took me to the hospital.

My stay at the hospital was one of learning more about my illness. A young Greek doctor found that the lithium carbonate that I had been taking most of the time since age 21 was attacking my urethral duct, which leads out of the kidneys. He immediately changed me over to Depakote which is a drug used mostly for seizures but also for Bi-polar I Disorder. During the three or four weeks that I was in the hospital I fell on a wet floor on my back in the corridor 3 times. Satan was not happy with what was to happen next.

My roommate at the hospital was about 10 or 15 years younger than me. She took an immediate interest in me and wanted to know what I was about. I freely ministered to her and she drank it in like a sponge. She gave her life to the Lord Jesus and was so excited she could barely contain herself. I showed her in the Bible to read certain passages first like the gospel of John. She was a transformed person! Her appreciation of me was great and we had some sweet fellowship together before she was discharged. Australia is a land on the verge of great revival. The huge church, with Houston as pastor and Darlene Zschech as worship leader, was used by God to bring Christians into intimate worship. It's too bad that I didn't get to stay the full three months and experience that great ministry.

The doctor sent me home a couple of weeks early. He and the nurses were so helpful to me! They gave me good care and I was never billed at all! A nurse accompanied me to the airport to make sure I got on the right plane. I was able to sleep on the return trip because of Ativan, a sleep aid. When I got to St. Louis I called my son, David and he and his girlfriend came to pick me up. He was doing well except not in college due to some trouble he got himself into. He soon got a good steady job at Babies R Us where he worked for several years. Then the next semester he started on his associate's degree at Meramec College. A so-called friend took his beautiful white Infinity sedan and totaled it. Such is the life of a teenager. He became more sober and used a little more wisdom in choosing his friends after that. While David was maturing the Lord was moving me to a place where I could make it and soon a series of events took place.

First my Depakote wasn't strong enough in my system yet and I got very sick. When I went to the psychiatrist I broke down and cried. The tears came and I couldn't stop crying. She called an ambulance and they took me to the hospital. Since I lacked funds I was at the state hospital on Delmar. It was quite an experience. After my medicine got regulated I felt great and went about trying to help others. My doctor said that I should have been a doctor because of my heart to come to the aid of everyone. Well, when they discharged me I had nowhere to live so my social worker looked around for a group residential care facility. The only one with an opening in St. Louis smelled like urine. So, she ended up driving me south where she found one in Festus. I felt like in the bible when it says that they would take Peter where he didn't want to go. Yet God was giving me a place where I could make it and have a new beginning.

God says in Hebrews 11:32-34

*"Remember those earlier days after
you had received the light, when you stood your ground in
a great contest in face of suffering. Sometimes you were
publicly exposed to insult and persecution; at other times
you stood side by side with those who were so treated. You
sympathized with those in prison and joyfully accepted
the confiscation of your property, because you knew that
you yourselves had better and lasting possessions." God
says in Heb. 10:32 "So do not lose the courage you had in
the past, which has great reward. You must hold on, so
you can do what God wants and receive what he has*

promised. For in a very short time, The One who is coming will come and will not be delayed. The person who is right with me will live by trusting in me. But if he turns back with fear, I will not be pleased with him. But we are not those who turn back and are lost. We are people who have faith and are saved."

Keaton Center is the place God provided for my safety for two years. It is owned and operated by Comtrea. When I was there, the director was not a Christian and she didn't like me. It was a controlled environment and had so many rules. One was that you had to stay six inches away from one another. That was hard for me because I am affectionate and love to give and receive hugs.

Hugging

The Surgeon General recently announced that hugging is n excellent health promotion activity. In the Surgeon General's recently published five volume, 5,234-page report, researchers conclude that hugging is, non-fattening, naturally sweet and contains no artificial ingredients. It is wholesome and pure, and most important, fully returnable.

The food was fattening. They served a lot of fried foods and starches. In order to keep my health, I joined the YMCA and worked out 3 times a week. Because of a friend, Maria, from St. Louis I was able to keep my car. She gave her tithe to me for about a year and a half because she believed that God would use me to minister.

I started a Bible Study at Keaton Center but it ended up that only one woman came so it fizzled out after several months. During this time of waiting for my disability I worked part time for a home health care agency for the elderly out of Hillsboro. I was having severe sleep trouble and had to take a strong medicine to help me sleep. My roommate snored plus the lady on the other side of the wall snored and the wall right by my head actually vibrated! Some nights I didn't get any sleep leaving me with a severe headache the whole next day. But I learned not to burn bridges and to ride out the storm. God eventually sent me a roommate that didn't snore at all.

I also learned to trust God at a higher level than before. Sunday, July 23, 2000, Ginny at Vineyard Fellowship prophesied over me. "Tell Barbara not to fear the darkness around her. It is but a fleeting moment of time and this too will pass. I will pass my heart to her thoughts and she will be sustained. Come- come into the wholeness of who you are. Do not be afraid or doubt, Barbara, it only makes you stronger as you see the strength I have put in you to move mountains out of the way and take you into the truth of who you are in Christ Jesus. Your loving Father has heard your cries and is here to comfort you in your need. Fear not, Barbara, I never left your side for a moment. Trust me and believe as I am always your heart's desire. Your loving father in Christ Jesus."

Sunday August 13, 2000

A prophetess prophesied over me. "Barbara, I am bringing light to the darkness at Keaton Center. That I am his bride and God has separated me for a purpose. That I am a conqueror and will lead many to freedom." A little later she prophesied that many times the devil had tried to kill me but that God was giving him notice that day that never again would my life be threatened or in danger but that I would live. In October of 2000, a young lady from

Keaton Center poured out her heart to me and gave her life to Jesus!

As usual I was praying in a nearby park because in this case it was the only place I could sing in the spirit. When winter approached I got permission from 1st Methodist Church to pray there. Then in February I had a divine appointment that gave me a new opportunity. I was worshipping at Vineyard Fellowship on Telegraph Road in St. Louis and afterward I met a lady that told me about Proceeding Word Ministries in Festus. She said that they had cell groups and to check it out. So I did, the next Sunday. Pastor Everett gave me a key to the church so that I could pray whenever I wanted to. I liked that little fellowship and they loved me so I started going there in February of 2001. Another advantage is that I could walk there. It was about 5 minutes from Keaton Center!

17

4 years old
I'm washing dishes and David
Comes up behind me and was
pulling up my nightgown...
"Momma, I'm going to pull off your CURTAIN."

About that time my disability came through and I started looking for an apartment. Festus Gardens seemed to be the place best for me and my pocket book so I got on the waiting list. It took a year before I was accepted and the phone call came and boy was I excited to get out of the group home! The move went smoothly with Pastor Everett and some of the members of the church helping me. My furniture had been stored in my friend Marilyn's basement for over 2 years. My apartment was nice, perfect for me!

In March of 2002 my mom died. She had Alzheimer's for years. Then within two months dad died. Before their deaths I had driven back and forth from Festus to St. Louis helping out as best I could. I gave my mom her showers and cut her hair and later fixed dad his lunch and helped with the laundry. But because of the strong medicine I was on, and the stress, I had a very scary experience. I was driving from my son David's apartment in Mehlville to go home and on the ramp leaving 270 and entering 55 south, I went blind on the cloverleaf. Just like in Carrie Underwood's song: "Jesus take the wheel," I cried out, "God drive this car!" Miraculously I was able to make the curve by gradually turning my wheel. I realized that I was under too much stress but God promises not to give us more than we can handle.

Then my minister's wife died in September. She was greatly missed by our congregation. Before she died she prophesied over me that I was like Enoch and that God would use me as a general in his army. I knew that I needed to get off my sleep medicine in order to minister in that kind of power. Also my intimacy with God would have to be restored. Since I moved into my own apartment I now had an opportunity to spend time alone with the Lord. The park across from Festus Gardens Apartments was a very good place to start, although I had a close call in Sunset Park a few years before. I was interceding for America and two policemen came up to me asking me, "what are you doing?" I said. "I'm praying." There was complete silence. One of them asked for my ID. I didn't have it on me because I had walked to the park. Then to my relief the policemen said, "Pray for me, pray for me!" Then they left. I learned to always have my driver's license on me even if I was just taking a walk.

As far as my medicine and getting off of the high powered Zyprexa, I had to make a decision. Medicine is like a Band-Aid. It helps the symptoms but doesn't heal the root problem. I was able to get off of Zyprexa but was still on much more mild sleep help. God alone could heal me of the trauma of so many years. He would have to teach me to sleep again. What helped more than anything was exercise. I continued to dance unto the Lord in my living room and still used my scholarship at the YMCA in Festus to stay in shape and jog to get my endorphins going. Sometimes I looked forward to sharing my gift of dance with others. In 1995 I had gotten to dance at my mom and dad's retirement home, the Villas of Tesson Ferry. The program lasted 45 minutes and it was a mixture of Christian and secular music. Barbra Streisand's "You Don't Bring Me Flowers" was their favorite. My mom and dad cried through over half of my performance. The audience was greatly moved by the Christian dances. I was thrilled for the opportunity. I had never seen my dad cry before. My mom wanted me to dance again. The next day my legs felt like rubber bands and drained. I hadn't danced that long for a great many years.

During these critical years God gave me some precious friends. Kathy and I started praying together at Proceeding Word Ministries in the winter of 2001. She and I would intercede for our children especially, but also the whole church and the world. We are still close friends. We go charismatic shopping. That's what I call it because whenever we get together and shop God leads us straight to what we want and we are finished with plenty of time for a nice lunch and time of fellowship.

One morning at the YMCA I was getting ready to jump into the shower but realized that I couldn't read the writing on my shampoo and conditioner bottles without my glasses. A nice lady helped me by telling me the difference between the two and I was appreciative. We fell into a conversation and she and I were best friends until she passed away a year ago. Diane taught aquatics classes at the YMCA. We had so much in common! Our sons are about the same age and she loves the Lord. Diane helped me through some rough times and was always there to listen to me. She accepted my mental illness. One day I was manic because I hadn't slept a wink the night before and I got as nutty as a fruitcake. We were sitting on a bench in the locker room. She laughed along with me. I thought I'd never wind down. Diane was loved by me and all the Y members.

About this time, "The Passion," a movie directed by Mel Gibson, came out in the theatres. Our church went as a group and something awesome happened. During the previews the electricity went out and the room went black. One of the attendants came in to tell us to stay in our seats. We all waited patiently. Then after a few minutes a group of African Americans began to worship God in songs. Many joined in. The music was beautiful! Then a couple of attendants said they would give rain checks so we could come back another day. Nobody moved. After about 45 minutes total, Phil, one of Proceeding Word Ministries church members, stood up and led us all in prayer, simple but powerful. The lights came back on and the movie began. Everyone cheered. We serve an awesome GOD!

The Passion of Christ was tear jerking, heart wrenching and so intense and bloody. I had to close my eyes for some scenes. If one is not convinced of Christ's love for us after seeing "The Passion" they are so blinded by Satan or their hearts are too hardened to believe. Phil reminded me of a quote and scripture: *"Only one out of an entire crowd is daring enough to invest his faith in the character of God."*

"God's eyes go to and fro upon the earth   seeking to show himself
        strong on the behalf of them whose heart is perfect toward him."

II Chron. 16:9

Purity + Prayer = Power
Desire + Discipline = Delight
Whatever our source will determine our course!
He is no fool who gives what he cannot keep who
gives his life for free.

*"He who loves a pure heart and whose speech is gracious
will have the king for his friend."* Pros. 22"11

Where there is faith
There is hope.
Where there is hope
There is love.
Where there is love
There is peace.
Where there is peace
There is God.
Where there is God
There is no need.

"God permits what he hates to achieve what he
loves." -Joni Ereackson Tada

When I was at the group home I tried so hard to
work and get my body tired in order to sleep. My part time
job was perfect for me, caring for the elderly in their homes,
but they didn't have many clients to give me. So I decided
to go with volunteer work. I went to Jefferson Memorial
Hospital and became an escort. It was easy, fun and
rewarding to help the sick. When it got a little boring I
decided to make a change. Crystal Oaks Nursing Home
next door became a great place for me. I was able to use my

art talent dancing and even preaching. The activity director, Michelle, took a liking to me and we had fun. One Wednesday morning after I finished ministering to the elderly, almost all in wheel chairs, a lady asked me, "Who ordained you?" I said to her. "I'm not ordained," She said, "Oh yes you are." Later, on another occasion, she said, "I want to know who ordained you." I told her, "I'm not ordained by man." God ordained me. It's obvious to those who really know me. My ministry at Crystal Oaks was like a breath of fresh air. God had given me a green pasture time. How thankful I was! Not only did I get to preach, but I led the singing and gave each person an opportunity for one on one ministry afterward. Plus I gave anyone who wanted one a shoulder massage. Almost all of them loved that personal touch. The elderly in homes are starved for love and I naturally met that need yet, out of the blue I was replaced. I don't know why and I never asked. Just when I got something perfect going, oh well!

Personal Prophecy

Christian International Versailles Indiana
January 24th, 2003

Barbara when you stood up I heard the Lord say "wow!" I asked the Lord what did that mean. She's a woman of worship and the Lord said, you're one that has worshiped much that knows the ins and outs of worship, the benefits of worship. You're one that's heart can cry out to me, and worship even when you're in surroundings with other people and they don't even know that you are worshiping. The Lord says I know you're worshiping. I hear your cries of worship. I see your cries of worship and daughter because of that I have much reward for you and this is a year of breakthrough for you and the Lord says, I say back to you wow! Because I am going to wow you in this year the Lord says, Things that you have prayed for your whole life you're going to see come to pass this year and daughter I want you to know when you see them start to happen it's because you have been a worshiper unto me and the Lord says I'm going to raise you up to the next level now and I'm going to put you in a place where you're going to be able to teach worship, model worship, example worship, and bring other people into worship. Daughter, this night I am placing a new mantle of worship and everywhere you go you are going to take it with you and that you're going to have people around about you just fall on their knees and repent and get right with me daughter just because your heart is so closely knitted to mine and my presence is so greatly upon you and the Lord said, when you chose to worship, daughter you chose the right thing.

You're the one who has stood in the gap for people and not always, not always things have broken through for you. I heard the Lord say tonight that he himself is going to stand in the gap for you and there are going to be miracles and you're going to see things throughout this year.

I hear as you see the miracles, it's going to put even a stronger backbone of steal within you and you are going to get a boldness and you're going to step forward even more in areas that you have not been making declarations and declaring woo to the enemy but you had just been worshiping and praying. The Lord is going to take you into a new dimension with that because as you see the answer to the prayers and the miracles that you're going to get a boldness to get into a different warrior intercession that you have not been in before.

We seal this word over Barbara. We send her out with a higher level of worship, miracles manifesting while she worships and we pray that you strengthen her, we rebuke fear off of her and we just thank you that the gifting will come forth in Jesus name. Amen.

Monday January 27th, 2003

My sister, Sally, came over for lunch and for me to show her around Festus. Her hand had been badly damaged by overwork on her kitchen floor sealant. She couldn't put her fingers together and had no strength in her hand. She had gone to the doctor and he told her just to rest it but it wasn't getting any better. Sally asked me to pray for her hand. I got out some anointing oil and put a cross on her forehead and said a simple prayer of faith. She immediately could put her fingers together and began flexing her hand. Strength came back into her hand! When she left she thanked me for lunch but especially God's Healing.

Our little church continued to love me and our cell group was so supportive! Pastor Everett taught us many helpful applications to life. One was the:

<u>Dance of Fear</u>

1) One gets hurt
2) It creates a need or want
3) Then fear creeps in
4) One reacts to that fear

The reaction causes problems and if a married couple dances to dance of fear together then it makes it more complicated and dangerous. There is a book out about the fear of rejection. John Bevere writes about the spirit of offense being the bait of Satan. The mentally ill get offended often, because they are misunderstood. Sometimes they experience things like: hallucinations, panic attacks, paranoia, etc. When we have fears they are really:

F-false
E-evidence
A-appearing

R-real

Or David once told me

F-forgetting
E-everything's
A-all
R-right

We must throw off those fears and replace them by the
Word of God or Truth.

Our church said we should have the momma-bear
mentality protecting our youth. Another thing I have
learned is that everyone has ungodly beliefs. They are
conclusions we make because of something that has
happened to us like. "I will always have financial
problems." Then the Bible says that *"My Heavenly Father
will supply all my needs according to His riches in glory by
Christ Jesus." Phil. 4:19* " My earthly father disappointed
me, my earthly husband disappointed me, but my
Heavenly Father will never disappoint me."

Satan tried to get me to doubt God and get confused
about what the Heavenly Father was doing in my life. If the
group home was not enough to cause total despair he
thought he could destroy me in a different way. I had been
working part time at Immanuel Lutheran's Day Care
Center but because of sleepless nights I was unable to keep
up with all the work they piled on me. I decided that job is
more for younger ladies. One good memory is that Kelly, a
coworker, got healed of lung cancer after I anointed her
with oil and prayed for her. God is good! Don't get me
wrong, I'm sure other people were praying for her also.
When I lost my job at the Lutheran church, I felt displaced

and lost. Emptiness swept over me and I really had sleep trouble. I went to the YMCA to see if they would let me help teach ballet. But you had to be able to teach jazz, pom-poms and tumbling in addition to ballet so that was a closed door. Little did I know that God was opening a new door for me that was right up my alley. I talked to Karen at the YMCA and told her that I wanted to use my gift of dance to bless the YMCA. She referred me to Katrina, one of the ballet teachers in the dance department. I set up an interview for Thursday night. It was on Sunday before my interview that prophet Knight, a lawyer and prophet who grew up in Africa with missionary parents, came to our church. He didn't know me from Adam and he told me, "Daughter you will be teaching worship dance to teenagers." That Thursday night Katrina watched me dance and said, "Wow, I can tell that you've been dancing all your life, you're hired!" Glory to the almighty God!

God gave me a special friend to dance with. She is full blooded Italian and she is young enough to be my daughter. She is petite and has long black hair. We enjoy each other and share our gift of dance at the YMCA. She teaches me the newer style of ballet, while I tend to stick more with the classical form. I'm never depressed when I'm dancing with this cute girl that God brought into my life.

Feb. 24, 2004, which was my late husband, Paul's birthday, I started teaching Christian expressive dance to the staff and 3 teenagers in the multi-purpose room at the YMCA. Prophet Knight's prophecy had come true! I had one teenager that was a very good dancer. She was thrilled and just took off making all the turns and flowed. One day I walked into the weight room and she threw her arms around my neck in appreciation for teaching her this new kind of dance. Joy flooded my heart. I was making a difference in lives and that's what I'm here for! It's hard to give up such a fun job but in the end I had to. Again sickness struck me. I was hospitalized and my medicine was imbalanced. Someone once told me that a curse like my mental infirmity is empowerment to fail. I believe that because I have lived it. What could get me over this dilemma? I searched and searched for the answer and I discovered that the Word of God was the only thing that would work against such a powerful enemy. Dealing with my manic state has been so difficult that knowing the Word of God is not enough. I have to meditate on it and eat it to help it to take over my mind. Some people call it the renewing of the mind. My friend Christie in St. Louis mailed me a book called "Meditation" where I lived at Keaton Center. It is the key to success for all Christians.

One scripture that helped me the most is "Be Still and Know." Someone told all of us at church to just "crawl up into Jesus' lap and let Him love you. Rest, do nothing except what Jesus wants you to do. Don't do it alone. Jesus sent out in two's." I also had to meditate on The Song of Solomon and roll over my adoration and faithfulness of my precious Paul to Jesus. It wasn't easy and during my struggle I found myself having more sleep trouble. When I left Paul I gave up my world, my hero, my attachment, my leader, the love of my life. My heart was still forever toward Paul. I was doing the best I could; yet I was drowning in the past. I needed a break, a vacation. So I called my good friend Coleen and asked her if I could visit her. She said yes. She has the gift of hospitality. We hadn't seen each other for years and we still picked up where we left off. Our fellowship was sweet. During one of our prayer times she said that she heard the word "Fear." I didn't think I had any. As I searched my heart I realized that I was afraid of not sleeping and going into unreality.

110

Paul's and my relationship proved its intimacy and intensity of both agony and elation. What do we do when we can't explain what God is doing? Will we remain nearby when He hasn't stopped a tragedy? That's what makes us different! I recalled another friendship in the past, a young lady, Maria. My whole time at Keaton Center she had come to visit me bringing her tithe to me. Why? Because she believed in me, that I was making a difference among the mentally ill. She and I had grown close from all the long walks we had taken together at Jefferson Barracks Cemetery. I was a mentor to her and I couldn't let her down. I also remembered what Kathy had told me. She said I have a special anointing on my life as I listen to people. All my life since age 15, people come up to me and easily pour out their life's troubles to me. While walking the track at the YMCA, those in need stop me or come up beside me and tell me what is on their heart. I love to listen and they sense it. Sometimes I pray with them on the spot and God heals right then or maybe a little later. It was my time to be healed of the fear of going into unreality.

After visiting Coleen at the Lake of the Ozarks, I was determined to deal with this fear. God was meeting me right where I needed him. But first I would be challenged to the hilt! After 9 months and 8 hospitalizations I realized that I was not healed of the past. The sleeping medicines I was on were out of balance and I lost my footing. It was as if I was a ping pong ball bouncing back and forth between the hospital and home. My doctor got put out with me and said that he wouldn't see me any more unless I became a ward of the state. I told him to call the doctor at the stress unit at the hospital. He didn't do it. So, in 2005 right before Magnolia House, I decided to get shock treatments. Maybe that could help me forget the past long enough to deal with the present. They gave me three per week for 2-3 weeks in

January of 2005. They seemed to help me but I had to lose my apartment and go into another group home.

About this time I was watching the Christian TV and TD Jakes was preaching: "What to do when you don't know what to do." He said, "God's will does lead to valleys. Pull things together, don't be scattered. God won't fix for you what you can fix yourself. When life asks you a question 'Can these bones live again' (Ezek. 37) speak to those things that are not, prophesy, talk to the future as you are commanded. Obey God and things will snap in line. Act on what you've been taught. God's Word works! Consider every area of your life that is scattered. Lord, teach us to number our days and to make every moment count." What a mighty man of God! Another thing that helped me is my application of "Breaking Free," a Bible study written by Beth Moore. She talks about setting one's self free from lies of the devil by identifying the lie then putting a truth from the Bible in its place. I did this in regards to my mother-in-law and it worked! She passed away in September of 2004, a tremendous loss to me. We were very close even after my divorce from her son in 1989.

18

4 years old
David is playing in the den,
he decides to change into his overalls.
As he hammers on his toy work bench,
he says over and over and over again,
"Workman for my Lord"

In August of 2004 I lay on a gurney at Jefferson Memorial Hospital. I had taken or mixed sleeping medications and was in a very bad way. My mind was under attack and I was in trouble. I just remember laying there separated from everyone. I begged the nurse to hold my hand. She took it and patted it and told me that she had to go. The lights in the emergency room were bright and I needed to sleep so badly. All of a sudden I felt completely separated from God and without hope. I had never felt such a horrible condition in all my life. I was petrified and glued to the bed. For a period of several long minutes I was in Hell, at least I felt like it. People were coming in and out of the emergency room but I was all alone, isolated and frightened. Finally they came in and gave me a shot of Ativan. Then I was helped into a wheelchair and pushed up into my room. I woke up the next morning with a sigh of relief. I wasn't in Hell. I was in the stress unit!

In the July 29th entry of "My Utmost for His Highest," Oswald Chambers writes: "In the Bible clouds are always associated with God. Clouds are the sorrows, sufferings, or providential circumstances, within or without our personal lives, which actually seem to contradict the sovereignty of God. Yet it is through these very clouds that the Spirit of God is teaching us how to walk by faith. If there were never any clouds in our lives, we would have no faith. ` The clouds are the dust of His feet.' (Nahum 1:3) They are a sign that God is there… Through every cloud He brings our way, He wants us to unlearn something. His purpose in using the cloud is to amplify our beliefs until our relationship with Him is exactly like that of a child- a relationship simply between God and our own soul, and where other people are but shadows… Until we can come face to face with the deepest, darkest fact of life without damaging our view of God's character we do not yet know Him."

On Sunday, May 23, 2004 I was greatly encouraged by a personal prophecy given to me by Tim from Versailles, Indiana. He said, "Father we bless Barbara, we thank you for the stirring in her heart for intercession that it be called forth right now in the name of Jesus. I see prosperity and blessing all over you. Father, I thank you for the anointing of God for this daughter of Zion even this night these limits are being broken sayeth God and they are controlled by even your lips and thought. I'm bringing you up to a new level of mindset that needs to be broken. Even tonight there's going to be a new activation, a dream that's going to be imparted into your heart, into you mind. There's going to be a new vision placed in front of you, a destiny is going

114

to be straightened out. For you didn't think past even 2 or 3 years. But oh daughter I have a plan for your life. I'm going to reveal this destiny unto you. It's going to include many things you have way deep down. You thought 'how could that be, God?" It will be so much fun and so simple, so easy, that's what I want to do. But that's what I put in you, saith God. I put that dream, that vision, that plan even within and now is the time you need to put legs on it, to implement it. Start putting it to work. You're going to find that very dream that I placed inside your heart many years ago is going to come out and is going to produce much for you. So draw close even unto me saith God. It's not going to be a work thing. It will produce money, supply. So be sensitive unto my heart and as you are sensitive you are going to see victory like you've never seen. Father, we release those things within her that tree, that vision, that goal that she had. We release that supernatural provision in Jesus' name.

June 18, 2004 I woke up early. When my feet hit the floor, God began speaking to me about my destiny. Then I went into an overwhelming time of weeping and repenting. One of my life's desires to unite the Body of Christ was urgent. God said that worship, dance, intercession, evangelism, and miracle power encounters are what it would take. My heart was so ready, so willing to do whatever it took to yield to God's will for my life. God was to teach me by taking me to a new level of peace around people that he needed me to be with to learn to enter into his rest.

In February of 2005 I moved into Magnolia Home. It was a quiet peaceful place. I had the whole upstairs to myself. It was a family owned and operated group home. We ate in a small dining room in close quarters so we learned to get along. The house was over one hundred years old and very homey. When I met Katherine, a lady about 90 years old, I felt so comfortable because she reminded me of my mother in law. She was a Christian and read her Bible and wholesome books. We talked every day and had a very close relationship. She wanted to go to heaven so badly that she begged God daily to take her home. The owner and operator of the home was a Christian and gave me permission to have a Bible study. So every Thursday morning we gathered together to learn from God's word.

As time went on we bonded together as brothers and sisters in Christ and evolved into a share group. We had men and women from many different backgrounds: Catholic, Baptist, Lutheran, Seventh Day Adventists, Presbyterians, non-denominational, etc. God was fine tuning my calling as he had showed me! Unite the body of Christ. While I was at Magnolia Home three people gave their lives to Christ and began living for Jesus! God was still working on me to truly enter into his rest. I had some close friends there, lots of laughs and some persecution. I would take long walks and sing outside in the alley. One of my favorite songs was "Without Him,"- "without him I could be nothing. Without Him I'd surely fail. Without Him I would be drifting like a ship without a sail." I danced and painted in the huge upstairs of that beautiful old house. I also had the opportunity to volunteer at the food pantry at the First United Methodist Church across the street. What a joy it was to give food to those in need and to pray with them. For the most part I have good memories while living there for 2 ½ years.

In the spring of 2007 I started volunteering under the activity director at Autumn Ridge Retirement Home in

Herculaneum, Mo. I just loved working under her. She was so creative, so versatile! After about 4 months they offered me an apartment on the 3rd floor in independent living. I had found favor with the Autumn Ridge staff! God had prepared me and then gave me the opportunity to have a larger place of ministry. It was as if God had opened up Heaven and dropped a gift in my lap! Thank you Jesus!

While there, I met a lady named Virgie and she and I hit it off right away. She and I are on the same page because we are intercessors and believe the Bible as it is written. She also is a lot like my precious mother in law. After several weeks at Autumn Ridge, I started an intercessory prayer group in my apartment. At first we had three, then five, and then we began meeting in the chapel in the lower level. We now have about 7 people. We have beautiful music, special times of sharing and pray for one another and others. God was with us in a very special way several weeks ago. Two ladies were crying so we started ministering to them and then many of us were crying. It was because we cared and were helping them as best we could. It was just like the early church in the book of Acts. The Holy Spirit was strong and the residents were so excited. They were talking about our time together throughout the week. Satan was jealous and decided to steal from us.

19

5 years old
I picked David up after his first day
of kindergarten. I asked him how many boys
were in his class. He said "eight".
Then I asked him, how many girls? He said, "Too many"!

Monday, November 17, 2008 the stock market had taken a plunge and I called my broker and found out how little I had in my trust. I knew it was coming because it's in the Bible about the last days. God says that He will take care of the lilies of the fields and they neither toil nor spin. God was bringing me to a higher level of trust. The Devil doesn't take control unless we let him. They say that fear weakens your immune system and it is true that perfect love casts out all fear. I was to confess my fear of uncertainty, proclaim the truth prophetically and give thanksgiving offerings to God for what He will do. Fear also breaks your will and paralyzes you.

Months before, the devil, had attacked me when coming home from a day with my friend. She had 3 hours of tests at the doctors and then we ate out. The day had gone well because we had quoted scriptures together between breathing tests and it helped the peace of God to flow between us. But when I walked through the door to the library at Autumn Ridge, a horrible dark cloud came from all around and gripped me. I could barely walk so I slowly made my way up to my 3rd floor room. I was glad that no one was around. When I got to my apartment I dropped my purse and staggered around begging God to show me what to do. I realized that I needed help so I went downstairs and asked a medical tech what to do. She said very kindly, "Barbara take your PRN (per request as needed) medicine, and we will go from there." Her calmness and compassion helped me so much! Although I was still overwhelmed by an evil force I made it safely back to my place. I took my designated amount of medicine as needed, grabbed my Bible and began reading Psa. 23 and on. At first I was still frightened and felt like packing my bag and going to the hospital. I decided to try and find my friend Virgie to pray with me. She was available and came to my living room. I told her what was happening and she prayed as best she knew how because she had a relative with bi-polar disorder. After she left I crawled up into my chair and read the scriptures and kept reading Psa. 33, a psalm of joy. I realized that a supernatural calmness had come over me. I got up and began to worship God and told the Devil where to go. Then I took a little more of my medicine and got ready for bed and slept like a lamb. The next morning I was fine.

When I told my friend Joan about what had happened, she gave me a statue of St. Michael the

Archangel who defends us in battle. She is Catholic and she has faith in God's protection over our souls. God has brought many people of the Catholic faith into my life in the past several years. Perhaps it's because my heart is like a Catholic. I laugh at myself, thinking, and "I have a Catholic heart, charismatic feet and Methodist hands." The Methodists are great doers of the word. God is uniting the body of Christ although it isn't truly evident yet.

I began studying worry which is a form of rebellion because we are not trusting fully in God. It is a form of fear, so is dread, anxiety and qualms. I must not dwell in the past which is one reason I am writing this book: to get healed of the past and move forward. Holy fear of God comes as we encounter with God. A visitation: a vision, dream or the presence of God coming on us that one experiences the reality of God's holiness. Faith is what pleases God and brings his promises to pass. God works best in abundance. Let it flow!

Victory Over Fear Prayer

Father, in Jesus name, I confess and believe that "no weapon formed against me shall prosper, and any tongue that rises against me in judgment, I shall show to be in the wrong" Isa. 54. I believe. "I dwell in the secret place of the Most High. I shall remain stable and fixed under the shadow of the Almighty God whose power no foe can withstand-this secret place hides me from strife of tongues".

Declaration

I confess and believe the wisdom of God's Word dwells in me, and because it does, I realize that I am without fear or dread of evil. In all my ways I know and acknowledge God and His Word. Thus,

He directs and makes straight and plain my pathway. As I attend to God's Word, it is health to my nerves and sinews, and marrow and moistening to my bones.

I am strengthened and reinforced with mighty power in my inner self by the Holy Spirit Himself Who dwells in me. God is my strength and my refuge, and I confidently trust Him and in his word. I am empowered through my union with Almighty God. This gives me the superhuman, supernatural strength to walk in divine health and to live in abundance.

I take comfort and am encouraged and confidently and boldly say, "The Lord is my helper. I will not be seized with alarm. I will not fear or be terrified, for what can man do to me?"

God Himself has said, *"I will never leave you without support or forsake you or let you down, my child. [I will] not, [I will] not, [I will] not in any degree leave you helpless or relax my hold on you… assuredly not!" (Based on Hebrews 13:5* AMP)

Some manic moments are founded in fear and can be overcome. When fear starts to take hold of you immediately cry out to Jesus and focus on Him. Take control of your thought life. When I was 27 years old my doctor showed me how to do a type of meditation to help me to be calm. It helped tremendously! The key is breathing in through your nose and out through your mouth and counting your breaths. It works best when you are in a kneeling position facing a blank wall. My husband Paul would do it right beside me. We both benefited from this discipline. The scripture *"Be still and know that I am God." Psa. 46:10* is good to memorize and kept in your mind when in need of tranquility.

If you keep a tidy house it contributes to a tidy mind. When everything is in a place where you normally keep it, then you won't get flustered trying to find it. Then you can use your time to focus on the word of God, his desires for your life and giving of yourself and finances. Your priorities will fall into alignment and your mind can then be renewed and your life restored.

It is so important to live in the now. The past is a huge chunk of memory. Throw it away. Get set free! If you need help there are counselors and programs to help you. Our church has a ministry called "Celebrate Recovery" which is designed to help anyone with hurts, hang-ups and habits. I have been attending for a couple of years to get set free from my fear of insanity. I am on the worship team as a dancer and singer. I love to share my gifts with my friends as often as I can. Celebrate Recovery has given me a place of acceptance and I am thriving there. Being positive and receiving God's grace plus surrendering to God, resisting the Devil, he flies from me. I have learned to be aggressive on holiness by discipline.

The corporate anointing is coming...

Quiet times are important. Take time to listen to God. Meditate on who He is. If a scripture comes, look it up. Write down what he tells you. Isa. 26:3-4 *"He will keep in perfect peace all those who trust in Him, whose thoughts turn often to the Lord. Trust Jehovah as your everlasting strength."*

If you wake up in the middle of the night do mindless things like dusting then go back to bed and try to sleep. Or if you feel that God wants you to intercede for someone, pray. If you're hungry, eat a piece of fruit because it is easily digested. Don't worry if you can't sleep. Get up

122

and read or if your body needs rest, lie there and "play dead" (that's what I call it). I have started a Dream journal. God has been speaking to me a lot during the night.

One of the roughest times I ever had with not sleeping was when David was about 8 or 9. We were at my mom and dad's house and I went into a deep depression. I called my doctor telling him that I couldn't go on and he said to take my medicine and go to bed. So I did. There was a terrible thunderstorm and the sky was black although it was daytime. I just laid in bed feeling like I had no motivation to live. My mom came in and put a wet washcloth on my forehead then went back to her chores. Two or three days went by and I finally pulled out of it. At one point David had come up from playing in the basement. He looked at me and then at mom and dad. He was worried about me but didn't know what to say. Neither did I. But I pulled out of it and went back to work and God strengthened me for the task of raising my son. This prose helped me at this time.

Security

Isn't it good to know
When all roads are dead-ends
And all skies are overcast
And all dreams are nightmares
All hills are mountains
Isn't it good to know
When all faith has oozed out
And there is no place to stand.
That underneath are God's everlasting arms."
     W. Maurice king

This simple prayer helps me too. "God grant me crystal clear discernment and understanding directly from you. Control my mind Holy Spirit. Put me in your perfect peace and timing."

Many times I have to tell myself to relax. Here is an excerpt from "God Calling," May 18, 1988-Mother's day

The Rest of God

"I lead you. The way is clear. Go forward unafraid. I am beside you. Listen, listen, listen to My Voice. My hand is controlling all.
"Remember that I can work through you better when you are at rest. Go very slowly, very quietly from one duty to the next-taking time to rest and play between.
    "Do not be too busy. Take all in order as I say. The Rest of God is in a realm beyond all man's activities. Venture there often, and you will indeed find Peace and Joy.
    "All work that results from resting with God is miracle-work. Claim the power to work miracles."

"Know that you can do all things through Christ who strengthens you. Nay, more, know that you can do all things through Christ who rests you."
    Another helpful piece of advice is give anonymously to those in need and reap the rewards on God's terms. The Lord knows what you need before you even ask. One morning I looked down at my finger and realized that I had no silver bracelet to wear with Paul's Grandmas wedding ring. I thought to myself, "wouldn't it be nice to have one that would match my ring." That very night my family went to the fireworks at Webster Groves High School football stadium and as we were the first to arrive I noticed something on the bleachers. As I came nearer, I realized

124

that there were two silver bracelets lying on the seat. I tried them on and they fit perfectly! Isn't God awesome!

Keep busy; work as much as is possible even if it is volunteer work. Work is divine education, a part of God's discipline for the human race. There is a saying that goes: A person may do the work, but work makes the person. The Christian motive for working is to give and distribute. Christianity allows me to give to others what is rightfully mine. God has sovereign will, a permissive will and a protective will. Only God can lead us through the wilderness times in life right by our side as we yield to Him. It's then that we are content and trusting allowing us to prosper and gain in character. When God uses his protective will he will come in to block something in our lives to keep us out of trouble or even disaster. A good earthly father can help also like in the "Father Knows Best" TV show in the early 60's. The two children were disciplined when they needed to be corrected. Then they were pretty good kids and even helped some of their friends.

Change is difficult for the mentally ill. Remember that God is in control. When I'm in unreality, God is guiding me. The directive sovereignty of God means God knows the future. It's in sight and he has a certain time for everything. Eccl. 3:1-8 speaks of a *"weary round of life."* But it won't be like that in Heaven. We have abundant life now through Jesus. When we meditate on God's character, we lose our fear of everything. Those of us with mental illness in our families need to study and meditate on who God really is. To me, life is like a chess game. God makes a move, and then we make a move. He is such a patient Father that He will go around and around in the wilderness with us until we obey him. And remember godliness with contentment is great gain. God also has a permissive will and a protective will. He will come in to block something that He doesn't want to allow.

Obedience "submitting to God" triggers the release of God's resources.

"*Resist the Devil and he will flee from you.*" James 4:7. I was told one time to even laugh at the Devil. He only has power over us when we let him. Know your enemy but do not be enamored by him. Don't give Satan any credit or the time of day. That's just what he wants, attention. (Chris and Sue from my church prophesied over me that I would be doing some writing. I almost laughed because I am not a writer, another prophecy came true). Reverence for God is so very important. Psa. 56 is very encouraging:

"*God has removed my enemies. MY confidence is in Him alone. You are aware of my sleeplessness and have collected my tears in a bottle. In your book I cry out to you, Lord, and you answer 'God is for me!' I am not afraid of man. I will do what I have promised. I will walk before the Lord in the land of the living.*" Psa. 56:8

Know yourself and serve God out of that confidence. Know where you've come from, who you are and where you're going. Empty yourself, be a servant. God exalts obedience. God's way is perfect. Isa. 26:3. "*You will keep in perfect peace him whose mind is steadfast, because he trusts in you.*" I was praying one morning and said to the Lord: "God I have been praying so hard that my halo fell off." I laughed with Him.

And God said No

126

I asked God to take away my pride,
And God said "No."
He said it was not for Him to take away,
But for me to give up.
I asked God to make my handicapped child whole
And God said "No."
He said her spirit is whole; her body is only temporary.
I asked God to grant me patience,
And God said "No."
He said that patience is a by product of tribulation.
It isn't granted, it's earned.
I asked God to give me happiness,
And God said "No."
He said he gives blessings, happiness is up to me.
I asked God to spare me pain,
And God said "No."
He said, "Suffering draws you apart from worldly cares,
and brings you closer to me."
I asked God to make my spirit grow,
And God said "No."
He said I must grow on my own.
But He will prune me to make me fruitful.
I asked God to help me to love others,
As much as He loves me, and God said,
"Ah, finally, you have the idea."

Hebrews 12:1 "We have around us many people whose lives tell us what faith means. So let us run the race that is before us and <u>never give up</u>. We should remove from our lives anything that would get in the way and hold us back. <u>Let us look only to Jesus</u>

Take the limits off God! You can open the way for God to move on your behalf.

1. Fear of unknown
2. Doubt
3. Comfort Zone
4. Narrow-minded thinking
5. Past failures
6. Conditions not right
7. Logic says it won't work

Bipolar 1 Disorder

Bipolar I Disorder also known as manic depression is a serious medical condition which causes out of control changes in mood and energy. They are called episodes when one feels elated or low.

Genetics or heredity plays a role in mental illness. Personality types and stress seem to increase risk, frequency, and severity of the disease. Since I am a sanguine, with an outgoing personality, and also have a Holy Spirit controlled disposition my disease is harmless to me and others.

I have to deal with the extra energy as well as my normal athletic makeup. My mom said that I wasn't easy to get to sleep even as a baby.

The artist that I am, led me to find that such creative people as Italian artist Michelangelo, Danish fairy tale writer Hans Christian Anderson, German classical composer Ludwig Van Beethoven and American poet Emily Dickenson are all thought to have persevered with bipolar I disorder.

Some of the symptoms that I struggle with are: decreased need for sleep, talkative, racing thoughts or flight of ideas and increase in goal-directed activity.

With God's help I overcame depression in my early 20's. When I got filled with the Holy Spirit, like at Pentecost, I began dancing in the presence of the Lord. God inhabits the praises of the people!

There is no test, CAT scan, or other physiologic test that can diagnose bipolar I disorder. A diagnosis is usually made by health care professionals familiar with mental illness. With a Mood Disorder Questionnaire that the doctor uses they ask about your family history, what symptoms you've experienced, such as increased energy, decrease in sleep, taking risks then assess how much trouble these events have caused you.

I've always told my best friends how I feel so that they understand that my changes in mood are not my fault, but the result of a very real medical condition. They may even be able to recognize initial signs and symptoms before I do and help me to take steps to prevent an oncoming episode. I usually don't tell employers, co-workers or casual acquaintances of my disease.

For understanding, support and insight into your illness, connect with other bipolar I disorder sufferers. A peer group can be comforting and educational to share experiences and feelings. Your family and friends may also benefit from support groups offered by these peers.

Bipolar I Disorder usually requires lifelong treatment. The only cure for me is to know God. For me worshipping Him every morning along with prayer, Bible study, and meditation and doing everything God's way not mine is my salvation.

The good news is that I have overcome depression. Since I have taken much abuse all through my life, I still have insomnia. I also have a very sensitive chemical imbalance in my brain. The manic side of my illness is very tricky! My very awesome health care provider whom I prayed for 16 years is a Christian, young, intelligent, on the ball and compassionate person. She helps me in every way possible and usually trusts in my ideas about changes of medicine.

I took lithium from 1971 until 1999. It came out in 1970. Since the introduction of psycho tropics, these medications are often prescribed in various combinations to optimize a patient's treatment outcome.

Psychotherapy will help you if you choose. Your caregivers and family understand what sets off manic and depressive episodes of your disorder, so that you can cope more effectively.

Warning!! Be careful not to stop your medications before talking to your doctor. Halting medications may allow moods to once again swing out of balance. There may be more frequent and more severe episodes, leading to extreme risk taking, errors in judgment, hospitalization, or even suicide. This is very selfish and hurtful to the lives of people closest to you.

A healthy diet can improve how you feel and regular exercise can provide physical and emotional benefits. Learning to relax in times of stress and getting adequate sleep (my biggest challenge) can also improve your wellbeing. Doing productive things that you enjoy can help you to keep connected with your inner needs.

Dealing with anger is very important! Anger turned inward is depression. The word of God says to be angry but to sin not. How do we do this? Pray and keep in the power of the Holy Spirit who is the only one who can overcome life's temptations. The key is to know yourself and your warning signs. You might want to keep a mood or sleep diary to monitor your new stresses that may be causing feelings to erupt within you.

I almost always write down a list of things I want to ask my psychiatrist. Since I only see her every other month it is important to keep up with all changes.

When I feel anxious or overwhelmed I ask myself: What is the source? What will it take for me to overcome this?

The Power of Change

of Faith

of Prayer/Praise

of Hope

I remind myself, I'm not alone. Depression affects about one out of every ten people in America. It's not in my head. Depression can cause physical pain too. Headaches are worse when you're manic. They are severely painful, almost like a migraine headache.

Neurotransmitters regulate wakefulness and our body's dealing with arousal. They are the molecules that carry signals between neurons (nerve cells) at synapses in the nervous system. There are three major groups: amino acids, peptides and monoamines- insulin and zinc. The receptor is what dictates the neurotransmitter's effect. Nor epinephrine effects wakefulness or arousal. Dopamine effects emotional arousal. Serotonin effects memory, emotions, wakefulness, and sleep and temperature regulation. These elements bind to receptors. Molecular neuroscience is helping us to understand how to help the mentally ill. Nerve impulse receiving neuron glutamate is the most common excitatory transmitter. Endorphins lift moods. That's why dancing and aerobics are so valuable to me.

What we eat is of great value to the mentally ill. My psychiatrist gave me a book when I was in my late twenties that helped me a great deal with nutrition: Ortho-molecular Nutrition New Lifestyle for Super Good Health by Abram Hoffer, PhD, M.D. and Morton Walker, D.P.M. Orthomolecular nutrition is the ingestion of the optimum level of each nutrient for each individual. No one lives in a perfect environment. God has evolved nature to have a complicated set of checks and balances so such quick growing organisms run into the reality of a limited environment.

Corrective nutritional therapy can help overcome the effects of poor nutrition. Most psychiatrists don't get into good nutrition unless they have suffered themselves with psychological manifestations. There is nothing more convincing as a personal cure, especially when every other treatment has been ineffective. When I was in my late twenties I attempted to be a vegetarian and it seemed to help. The problem was that we kept moving so often that I got discouraged trying to buy healthy foods in small towns we lived in. One time my psychiatrist's wife got mad at Paul and threw up her hands and said "Are you moving her again?" All the changes were taking a toll on me. So I simply got away from refined carbohydrates and tried to eat a low fat diet. Plus my psychiatrist taught me a mental relaxation technique and gave me vitamin C and B complex shots if I had a bout with my illness.

Vitamin B-3 was recognized as a vitamin in the mid 1930"s. It is also called nicotinic acid. The two chemical properties are nicotinic acid and nicotinamide. This acid is often referred to as niacin or niacin amide. Niacin amide is generally used for treatment since the burning, flushing and itching of the skin that frequently accompanies nicotinic acid does not occur. Since this acid is not free but bound in foods, I take the slow released supplement. Nicotinamide is a form of vitamin B-3 that does not produce a flush, is alkaline and induces no acidity in the stomach. B-3 is important for the treatment of mental illness because of the effects on complex chemical interactions that affect the workings of the nervous system. The way other B vitamins and especially vitamin C and minerals are found in natural sources are listed in the book mentioned above. For example, B-6 is found in meat, fish, wheat germ, egg yolk, cantaloupe, cabbage, milk and brewer's yeast. Then their functions and deficiencies are given; it aids in food assimilation and in protein and fat metabolism, prevents various nervous and skin disorders, and prevents nausea. A deficiency may result in nervousness, insomnia, skin eruptions, and loss of muscular control. Some foods eaten raw are said to pack purifying properties and act as antidotes against poisonous additives. There is a list of them on page 67 of the above mentioned book. Nutritive values of the edible parts of foods are found in Table II pages 102-103.

Because we lived in small towns which were not near big cities in South Georgia I wasn't about to get fully into the lifestyle of orthomolecular nutrition. One thing I do know is cutting back on sugar and caffeine helps the manic side of my illness. My doctor also taught me that if I got hungry during the night to eat a piece of fruit because it is easily digested.

One day God showed me three times how important omega 3's and raw vegetable are for our brains. I turned on my T.V. that morning thinking that I had it on (Trinity Broadcasting Network) the Christian channel. Instead it was on channel 7. A doctor Unger was speaking about how the people in Iceland don't get depressed or have as bad of mood swings as people in the rest of the world. He also said that chromium helps too and has developed a mood enhancement formula. He also believes that our blood sugar level affects our moods. That afternoon I opened my Health for Woman magazine and it was all about D.H.A. (docosahexanica acid). This is an omega-3 fatty acid that if you don't have enough of it, you can develop nerve dysfunction (depression in some).

Of all the omega 3 in your brain and retinas, 97% are D.H.A. The three common omega 3's are ALA (alpha linoleic acid in foods like flaxseeds and walnuts), EPA (eicosapentaenoic acid found in cold water fish) and D.H.A. Some algae, which fish eat, have mainly DHA. How much evidence exists to show that DHA is a keep-em healthy ingredient for your brain, eyes and heart? There's enough evidence that it's only omega 3 foods additive approved for baby formula. This magazine recommends taking 600 milligrams of D.H.A. in food or supplements each day. That's the equivalent of 2 grams of metabolically distilled fish oil.

Then I opened to a health magazine that gave a list of fish as best sources of omega-3"s:

1.) Pollock
2.) Wild Salmon
3.) Black Sea Bass
4.) Atlantic Mackerel
5.) Rainbow Trout
6.) Artic Char
7.) Sardines
8.) Giant Perch
9.) Anchovies
10.) Black Cod
11.) White Sea Bass
12.) Bay Scallops
13.) Mussels
14.) Clam
15.) Dungeness Crab
16.) Oysters
17.) Striped Bass
18.) Pacific Sand Dabs

Understanding Triggers in the Brain
(Or: Healing the Broken Brain)

I.   **The Limbic System: Hard drive "platform"**

      A.   The Amygdala- the Body's "library" of emotional memories.

      B.   Hippocampus- The "Librarian" – retrieves memories from the Amygdala

      C.   Reticular Formation- "Netting" throughout this area that captures memories and causes new neural formation.

      D.   Thalamus- "Switching station" between the midbrain and the conscious brain.

E.   Hypothalamus- "Switching station" between the midbrain and the rest of the body — the thermostat.

F.   Other components of the Limbic System: Pleasure centers, drive our desires for sex, food, comfort; Basic motor functions of the body are controlled here too.

By 4 weeks gestation: Mid Brain Formation
By 5 weeks gestation: All parts of the Limbic system are present! Programming under way!
By 12 weeks gestation: Long term memory is already forming!

Whatever is in the Hard Drive will dictate how we perceive a stimulus. Whatever we see, hear, touch, taste, or smell, we *perceive* what our Hard Drives tells us to perceive!

II.   **Trigger Mechanisms: Superhighways in our brains**

A.   The Limbic System pathways — the Hard Drive Dictates to us:

- Self-Image
- Values and Priorities
- Attitudes
- Concept of God
- World View

B.   This results in how we conduct our lives:

- Our Income
- Perception of Opportunities
- Relationships

- Health and hardiness
- Leisure time activities
- Our niche in life (where we fit in)

C.   The Neural Pathways that have formed in our brains start out as "dirt roads."

    1.   Self-Talk forms more than 80% of our neural pathways in the Hard Drive.

    2.   The more we "travel down" a neural pathway, the more "paved" it becomes until it is a "superhighway."

    3.   Negative Neural Pathways can come to be the only road we travel, because it is a "superhighway"!!

D.   Events make new "roads" in our brain, and cause new emotional memories to be stored (like abuse, war, physical or emotional traumas, reactions to drugs).

- This new memory, when rehearsed, causes "feedback loops"
- These "feedback loops" change our thoughts and ultimately cause behavior patterns that are undesirable.
- These feedback loops cause chemical and electrical changes in the brain, as well as physical changes in the body, causing

mental illness, addiction, physical illnesses, and autoimmune disorders.

III.   **Trigger Mechanisms**

A.   Trigger Mechanism (TM): A Neural pathway resulting from a painful or traumatic event, which causes a foothold of the enemy and causes us to have patterns of negative emotions, poor health, and depleted immune systems.

B.   When this neural pathway forms, when something even benign or harmless happens that reminds us of this traumatic event, the hard drive causes us to react as if we have suffered trauma again.

1.   A child has unmet needs for nurturing. As an adult, he/she turns to porn, overeating, alcohol or attention-getting to attempt to meet those needs.

2.   Example: A woman is sexually assaulted by a hairy-chested man. Even watching TV, when she sees a hairy-chested man, she cannot watch the show anymore.

IV.   **Simple (Not "easy") Healing of a "Broken Brain"**

A. Ongoing *repentance, forgiveness, and deliverance* Mt. 4:24, Mk. 1:34, Mk. 3:15, Mk. 16:17-18

B. The Word: Prov. <u>4:22</u> The Word is HEALTH (lit. "Medicine") to a man's whole body! Rom. 12:2, II Cor. 4:16. By allowing the Word to get into our hearts, it brings the changes we need.

C. Discipleship: James 4:7 Submit to God, *then* resist the devil and he will flee! Mt. 28:19. The word "disciple" is where we get "discipline".

D. Prayer/Fasting: Fasting is used when prayer alone does not seem to work. Fasting "Looses the bonds of wickedness" (Isa. 58:6). Prayer is connecting to God, coming to him FIRST, so He can help us. As we behold Him, He *changes us from glory to glory!* (II Cor. 3:18)

V. **HOW TO DIFFUSE TRIGGER MECHANISMS:**

1. One category at a time: Think about the past event, when the emotion of this event is fully present, signal the prayer partner (hand squeeze, tap).

2. The prayer partner will say: **"I cancel and nullify the power of this experience and break the trigger (neural pathway) in Jesus' name",** and <u>clap</u> (this loud noise actually causes changes in the brain and helps to alter the pathway).

140

3.   The prayer partner will then pray and ask the Lord to establish new neural pathways and healing in the brain.

4.   Other components of healing include:

   a.   Forgiving the offender

   b.   Breaking soul ties

   c.   Confessing the Word related to this trigger to begin a new neural pathway to replace the old one.

Natural Care for Brain Function

Calcium/Magnesium: This blend acts as a relaxer—helps you rest. In addition, they are essential for muscle and heart function. Magnesium is also a natural Calcium 1200mg/Magnesium 500mg daily.

Co Q 10: Enhances Circulation, improves blood flow to the brain, improves cellular metabolism, making you feel great! 50-100 mg daily.

DHEA- Turns into glutathione in your body, which naturally detoxifies the body—eliminates poisons and heavy metals which inhibit brain function.

EFAs (Essential Fatty Acids): The brain is made of, essentially fat. Each nerve is covered with a fatty layer that acts as an insulator (like the covering on a wire). Only EFAs work. These are found in Fish Oil, Flax Seed oil and nuts and seeds. At least 1000 mg daily.

Ginko Biloba: Improves circulation thereby improving brain function and energy. NOTE: this also acts as a blood thinner. Do not take if you are on prescription blood thinners. Treats Alzheimer's, depression and migraines. 100-150 mg day.

L Glutamine: Increases muscle mass, improves mental function, natural treatment of both depression and schizophrenia. Up to 3 g/day.

L-Tyrosine: Enhances metabolism and thyroid function. Mood stabilizer. 500 mg 2x/day

Phosphatidyl Serine and Phosphatidyl Choline: Enhances memory and mood. These are enzymes that decrease with age. Take PC 25 mg day, PS up to 300mg day.

SAMe: This is an enzyme your body makes but decreases with age. This is the product of Choline (see above) and B vitamins. Take only if the vitamins don't work. This is a mood stabilizer (helps in depression and bipolar disorder) 200-400mg daily.

St. John's Wort: A natural antidepressant. Consult your practitioner before taking if you take an antidepressant. Takes about 6 weeks for full effect. 500-1000 mg daily.

Vitamin B12: Extremely important, enhances brain function among other things. Decrease with age. Sublingual is best. Up to 1000mg daily.

Vit. B Complex (Super B): This is essential for anyone over 40, or anyone who does not eat a balanced diet. B vitamins combine with homocysteine (BAD!) in your body to make stuff you really need (GOOD) for both brain and muscle function — prevents heart disease, nerve damage, gut problems, depression, anxiety…and on and on! One tab.

daily.

Vit. C: Bonds with lead in the body, then eliminates it. Lead causes brain damage, ADD, Alzheimer's, hallucinations and brain failures. Take 1000-3000mg day.

Vitamin D: Recent evidence shows that this vitamin prevents Alzheimer's, depression, Seasonal Affective Disorder, and other mental illnesses. Take 800-2000mg daily.

Zinc: An essential mineral for brain function. Research shows that people with diabetes, depression, ADD/ADHD, and Alzheimer's have a lack of it. Take 50mg daily, NO MORE THAN 100mg daily.

Other tips:

1. If it's white, don't eat it: White flour, sugar, potatoes, rice, breads. Whole grains only, replace white potatoes with yams, white rice with brown.

2. Avoid Aspartame (equal). It turns into formaldehyde in your body. It is a neurotoxin and destroys nerves! Use instead Stevia (truvia), which is a natural sweetener.

3. Sometimes we have hidden food sensitivities that can cause depression, anxiety, etc. Try eliminating suspect foods for 2 weeks, then eating them and observing your mood over 3 days after eating that food. IT can take up to 48 hours for a hidden allergic reaction to manifest. I did this and discovered I had sensitivity to white sugar (depression), which manifests 2 days after I eat sugar. This happens every time!

Avoid "junk foods." These have lots of additives that build up in your system, causing mood changes. Eat more whole foods like fruits and veggies, especially raw, like salads.

I WILL!

I WILL be strong in the face of weakness.
I WILL be brave in the face of fear.
I WILL persist in the face of failure.
I WILL stand again no matter how many times I fall.
I WILL follow my path no matter how often I lose my way.
I WILL live my dream no matter what obstacles stand
before me.
I WILL be mighty.
I WILL be bold.
I WILL be what God intended me to be.
I WILL!

One Church
Many Congregations

When we think about a big city — like Miami, for instance — we would say there are many different churches in Miami. But I don't think that is how God sees it. I believe God sees only *one* church. After all, the book of Revelation tells us Jesus is going to marry the Church — His Bride — and I do not believe Jesus is a bigamist. He's only going to marry one church. So we can think about many different churches, but God sees only one church. When Paul wrote his epistles, he didn't write to the Baptist church in Corinth, or to the Church of the Open Bible in Rome, or the Evangelical Church in Ephesus. He always wrote to the Church in the city. We are a long way from the reality of that today, but I don't believe God has ever changed His mind.

Therefore, I believe it is important that leaders of congregations within a city or region know how to relate to one another. It's very easy to become self-centered — to think about "my church" or "our church" and to focus on that alone. But that is not a scriptural attitude. I believe we as leaders should see one another as co-elders in the same church.

"We as leaders should see one another as co-elders in the same church."

"Therefore if there is any consolation in Christ, if any comfort of love, if any fellowship of the Spirit, if any affection and mercy, fulfill my joy by being like-minded, having the same love, being of one accord, of one mind. Let nothing be done through selfish ambition or conceit, but in lowliness of mind let each esteem others better than himself. Let each of you look out not only for his own interests, but also for the interests of others." (Phil 2:1-4)

Here, in his letter to the church at Philippi, Paul describes our attitude if we are to keep unity in the Body of Christ. He uses several different words, but there is one word that covers it all: humility. That's the key to unity. Proverbs 13:10 says *"Only by pride cometh contention."* (KJV) So it's logical that the opposite of pride — humility — would be the solution to contention.

The Bible teaches that while God may be forced to humble us, or we transgress and end up humiliated, He prefers that we humble ourselves. It is not something God desires to do for us. It's something we should do for ourselves.

Paul also said to let nothing be done through selfish

ambition. In my opinion, selfish ambition is the greatest single problem in the Church.

"Selfish ambition is the greatest single problem in the Church."

I've seen over the years many Christian ministers who are very insecure because their security depends on personal success. I have a different view of life altogether. For me, success is to please my Father. And security knows I am loved by my Father. I believe that's what the Gospel is intended to produce. Christianity is primarily about right relationships, not only right doctrine.

If every church leader and pastor in a city had as their primary motive to please the Father, there would be no rivalry. There would be no competition. I believe that is the way God wants us to live. I believe it's the answer for the question of Christian unity and ethics. If we get right with our Father, all other relationships will fall into place.

"Again I say to you that if two of you agree on earth concerning anything that they ask, it will be done for them by My Father in heaven. For where two or three are gathered together in my name, I am there in the midst of them." (Mt 18:19-20)

In the Greek, "agree" is a musical word. It gives us the word "symphony." It speaks about harmony. And Jesus says, "If two of you can harmonize on earth about anything that they ask, it will be done for them." I'm not a musician, but I do know that to be almost in harmony is very painful. I've seen many Christian relationships and church leaders that are almost in harmony. I think our broken relationships and lack of harmony causes God to stop up His ears in heaven.

--Excerpted and adapted from Derek Prince's teaching: The Ethics of Ministry." A longer version, "The Quest for

Character "can be read at www.dpmusa.org. Derek Prince (1915-2003) served as a founding board member of Intercessors for America.

Before I share the Gospel I like to ask the person, "Who is Jesus to you?" If needed then I ask them to "repent of your sins"

Give yourself to Jesus Christ and the blood will cover you.

Commit your way to the lord, trust also in Him, and He shall bring it to pass. –Psalm 37:5

"For God so loved the world that He gave His only begotten Son, that whoever believes in Him should not perish but have everlasting life."
-John 3:16

So they said, "Believe on the Lord Jesus Christ, and you will be saved, you and your household." –Acts 16:31

God Gives the Right to Be His Children

But as many received Him, to them He gave the right to become children of God, even to those who believe in His name.
-John 1:12

Confess Christ Openly

If you confess with your mouth the Lord Jesus and believe in your heart that God has raised Him from the dead, you will be saved. For with the heart one believes to righteousness, and with the mouth confession is made to salvation. For the scripture says, "Whoever believes on Him will not be put to shame." –Romans 10:9b-11

Integrity

We make a living by what we get. We make a life by what
we give. When we say no to the things of the world, we
open our hearts to the love of the Lord. "It's hard to
imagine the freedom we find from the things we leave
behind." Being one with yourself. -Michael Card